SHARES IN AMERICA

THE CASE FOR A UNIVERSAL BASIC INCOME

RICHARD FRENKEL

Hardback ISBN: 979-8-9944922-2-2

Paperback ISBN: 979-8-9944922-0-8

eBook ISBN: 979-8-9944922-1-5

Cover and interior design by meadencreative.com

First Edition

"The greatest source of instability in constitutions is the disproportion between rich and poor."

Aristotle, Greek Philosopher (c. 400 BCE)

"We may have democracy, or we may have wealth concentrated in the hands of a few, but we cannot have both."

Louis Brandeis, US Supreme Court justice (1856–1941)

"Would you accept an extra $12,000 per year for the good of your country?"

This book

CONTENTS

FIGURES

INTRODUCTION

The United States is one of the richest societies in human history. By almost any measure—output, productivity, technological sophistication—we are extraordinarily wealthy. If all the income generated each year were divided evenly, every household would receive over $190,000 per year, a comfortable living well above what most Americans actually earn. We produce more than enough for everyone to live securely.

Yet millions of Americans struggle to get by. Many work full time and remain poor. Others are one layoff, illness, or economic downturn away from crisis. Entire regions have been hollowed out by forces no individual worker caused and no amount of personal effort can reverse. At the same time, a small slice of the population captures an ever-growing share of income, wealth, and economic power.

This book begins with a simple question: If we are so rich, why does economic insecurity remain so widespread?

The usual answers focus on individual behavior, education, work ethic, and personal responsibility. But those explanations break down when confronted with the scale and persistence of the problem. Over the past two centuries, Americans have not become less industrious or less skilled. Quite the opposite. Productivity has exploded. Technology has transformed nearly every industry. We can produce vastly more with far fewer workers than ever before.

That success, paradoxically, is the root of the problem.

Modern economies no longer need everyone's labor all the time. Machines, software, automation, and now artificial intelligence steadily reduce the demand for human work, especially routine and middle-skill jobs. When productivity rises faster than wages, the economy grows while large numbers of people fall behind. The gains from growth increasingly flow to owners of capital and scarce skills, not to labor as a whole.

Our economic system still assumes that income must be earned primarily through employment. But employment is no longer a reliable or sufficient mechanism for distributing the wealth we collectively create.

The result is a system that works exactly as designed—and fails millions of people in the process.

Over the past century, the United States has tried to patch these failures with a sprawling collection of targeted programs: unemployment insurance, food assistance, housing subsidies, tax credits, disability programs, and dozens more. Many help, some work well, others poorly. But together they form a complex, stigmatizing, and often inadequate safety net - one that treats insecurity as an exception rather than a structural feature of a highly productive economy.

This book argues that we need to rethink the problem from the ground up.

Instead of asking how to create more jobs at any cost, or how to police the deserving from the undeserving, we should ask a more fundamental question: **How should the wealth of a rich, technologically advanced society be shared?**

Shares in America makes the case for a universal basic income—a guaranteed cash payment to every adult—as a direct, efficient, and dignified way to ensure that all Americans benefit from the nation's productivity. Not as charity. Not as welfare. But as a dividend from an economy built over generations by shared institutions, public investments, and collective knowledge.

A basic income would not replace work. It would recognize reality. It would provide a stable floor beneath everyone, reduce poverty and inequality, strengthen bargaining power for workers, simplify the safety net, and make the economy more resilient in the face of technological change.

Most importantly, it would align our system of income distribution with the world we actually live in, not the one we inherited from the industrial past.

This is not a radical idea. Versions of it have been proposed by economists across the political spectrum, tested in pilot programs, and quietly embedded in policies we already accept, from Social Security to Alaska's oil dividend. What is radical is continuing to believe that ever-increasing productivity can coexist indefinitely with widespread insecurity.

The United States can afford to ensure that no one falls below a basic standard of living. The question is no longer whether we can do it, but whether we are willing to share the gains of our collective success.

This book is about why we should—and how we can.

1

THE US IS A VERY RICH BUT VERY UNEQUAL COUNTRY

PRODUCTIVITY GROWTH MADE US RICH

Labor productivity measures how much labor it takes to produce something. A horse allows a farmer to plow a field far more quickly than by hand, thus raising the farmer's labor productivity—but only after the expense of buying and maintaining the horse. Likewise, a mechanical reaper dramatically increases the productivity of harvesting wheat, though it requires an up-front capital investment.

For most of human history, productivity improvements were modest at best. The modern era of rapid industrial productivity growth began around 1760, when the British developed machines to spin and weave cotton and powered them with water.

In both Britain and the United States, rising agricultural productivity paved the way for industrialization. In the British Isles, the introduction of potatoes and corn from the New World, the use of guano fertilizer, and improved farm machinery allowed fewer farmers to produce enough food to sustain a booming population—supplying labor for the new factories. In the US, inventions such as the cotton gin (1793) and the McCormick reaper (1831) revolutionized agricultural work. Westward expansion opened vast tracts of fertile land, and canals and railroads connected farms to markets. In the early 1800s, more than 80% of the US population worked in agriculture; today, only about 1% of workers do, even as yields per acre are far higher. This extraordinary increase in agricultural productivity fueled a mass migration from farms to cities and from agricultural to industrial work. Between 1800 and 1860, output per person doubled.[1]

After the Civil War, productivity in the US continued to climb with the spread of railroads, steelmaking, standardized parts, electric motors, and assembly lines. As in Britain, workers fought for better pay and conditions, while political corruption often favored wealthy interests. Immigration surged, preventing labor shortages and helping to populate the West.

....

1   The labor and growth estimates for 1800–1860 are from Thomas J. Weiss,1992, "U. S. Labor Force Estimates and Economic Growth, 1800–1860," American Economic Growth and Standards of Living before the Civil War, https://www.nber.org/system/files/chapters/c8007/c8007.pdf.

Mark Twain and Charles Dudley Warner captured the spirit of that period in *The Gilded Age*, a satirical take on an era of growth, greed, and speculation that gave the period its name. Yet the growth itself was very real: US GDP (Gross Domestic Product) rose from about $100 billion to $500 billion (in 2019 dollar-equivalent purchasing power) between 1870 and 1913. Average GDP per person more than doubled, from $4,590 to $10,373, despite a massive influx of immigrants from Europe that more than doubled the population.[2] Even so, wages remained low by modern standards—a laborer working 60 to 70 hours a week in 1913 earned roughly $15,000 a year in 2025 dollars, and most women did not work outside the home.

Growth continued through both world wars, but it was after World War II that productivity gains truly accelerated. Between 1950 and 2018, output per person quadrupled—from about $20,000 to $80,000 in 2025 dollars.

GDP per person and productivity are closely related. GDP is the total value of a country's final output in a year, while GDP per person divides that total by the population, including children and retirees. Productivity measures output per worker—or per hour worked. As output per work hour rises, GDP per person rises as well.

The figure below shows GDP per capita growth for groups of countries. The chart uses 2011 international dollars which are adjusted for both inflation and differences in purchasing power across countries.

2   Tables A1-c Angus Maddison, .n.d, "The World Economy: A Millennial Perspective," Oecd-llibrary.org, accessed February 24, 2022. https://read.oecd-ilibrary.org/economics/the-world-economy_9789264189980-en CPI adjusted from 1990 to 2019.

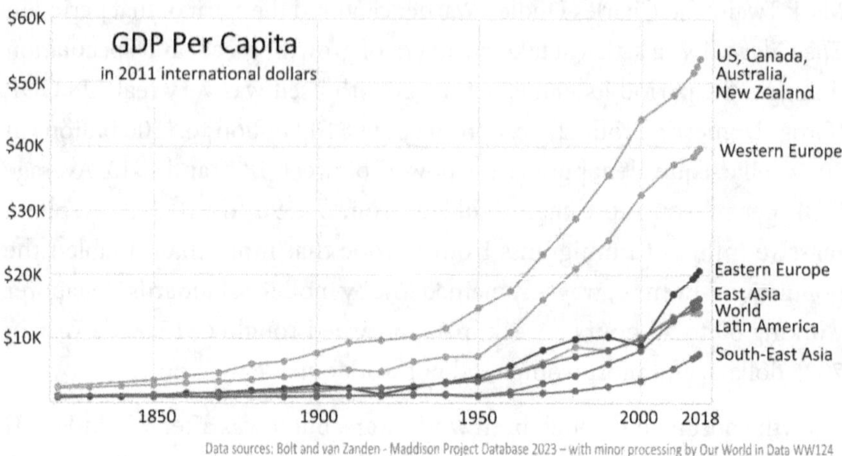

Figure 1. The Rise of Productivity. Amounts are adjusted for inflation and purchasing power between countries.

In late 2023, US GDP—our total output—amounted to about $203,000 per full-time worker. However, to sustain an economy, some portion of that output must be reinvested, since machines, buildings, and other capital assets wear out over time. The income that remains after accounting for this depreciation is called net domestic product or income. If all that net income in the United States were divided equally, each household of about 2.6 people would receive more than $190,000 per year as of 2024.

As I noted at the outset, the United States is an exceptionally rich country—and it achieved that wealth through enormous gains in productivity, or output per worker.

THE RISE AND FALL AND RISE OF US INCOME INEQUALITY

What can we say about the distribution of income and wealth in the United States?

The chart below shows the distribution of household income by decile in 2019.

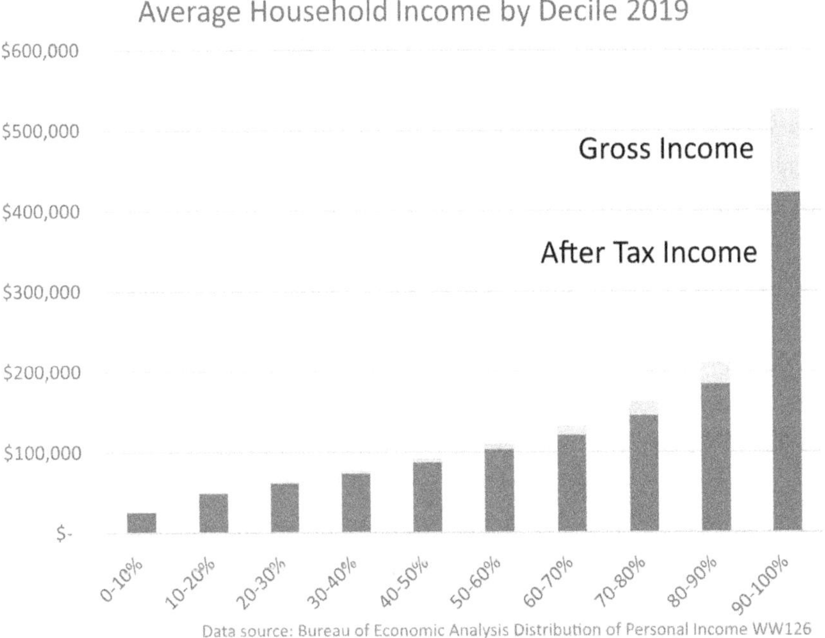

Figure 2. US Average Household Income. The horizontal axis is households group by income: For example, 0–10% means the 10% of households that make the least, while 90–100% means the 10% of households that make the most. Each group of 10% of households makes up a decile.

This chart includes all state, local, and federal taxes and transfers, but excludes capital gains. As the figure makes clear, the top decile stands out dramatically. Within that group, incomes are even more highly concentrated. The bar representing the top 1% would be four times as high as the top 10%

bar, and the top 0.01% bar would be 86 times as high.[3] That extraordinary concentration of income heavily skews the top decile upward. Today, the top 10% of households account for roughly half of all consumer spending in the US.[4]

Unequal distributions of income and wealth have always been the norm. For most of human history—and still in much of the world today—a small minority has owned most of the wealth and received a disproportionate share of income. The emergence of a large economic middle class was only made possible by the productivity discussed earlier. Yet technological progress alone was not enough; workers had to fight for a larger share of the fruits of that productivity.

The United States was something of an exception to income inequality in its early years. Economists and historians Jeffrey G. Williamson and Peter Lindert note:

> Colonial America was the most income-egalitarian rich place on the planet. Among all Americans—slaves included—the richest 1% got only 8.5% of total income in 1774. Among free Americans, the top 1% got only 7.6%. Today, the top 1% in the US gets more than 20% of total income.[5]

These authors show that income inequality in the US rose steeply between 1800 and 1860 with industrialization and remained high until World War II.

The next chart shows that coming into the twentieth century, inequality was extreme: The top 10% of households received about 45% of national income, while the bottom half received only around 15%.[6] During and after the Second World War, however, income inequality declined and the middle class expanded—a period sometimes called "The Great Compression" (a play on "The Great Depression") because the range of incomes narrowed significantly. What caused this unusual economic democratization?

....

3   The Distribution of Household Income, 2019, Congressional Budget Office. https://www.cbo.gov/publication/58353, Exhibit 1.

4   October 2025. https://www.marketplace.org/story/2025/09/17/top-10-of-earners-make-up-half-of-us-retail-spending

5   "Unequal Gains: American Growth and Inequality since 1700," n.d, CEPR, accessed June 9, 2025. https://cepr.org/voxeu/columns/unequal-gains-american-growth-and-inequality-1700.

6   Wealth distribution was, and is, far more lopsided. Three men in the US really do own more than the bottom half of the population currently.

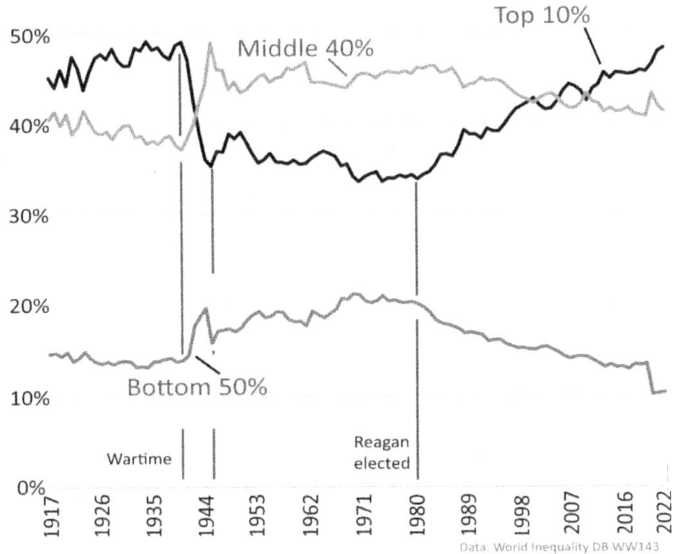

Figure 3. Percent of National Income by Income Group. The top 10% takes home 50% of national income, the middle 40% takes home 40% and the bottom 50% of households share what's left: 10% WW143

Part of the explanation is booming postwar demand. During the war, government-imposed wage and price controls, along with massive industrial mobilization, limited consumer spending. Much of the industrial sector was converted to supplying war materials: General Motors became the world's largest military contractor and did not make a single car between early 1942 and late 1945. The US supplied not only its own armed forces but also the Allies, with Britain and the Soviet Union borrowing heavily from the US to fund their purchases. Domestic rationing further curbed consumer demand, pushing the personal savings rate to nearly 30%, compared with about 5% today.

When the war ended, this pent-up demand and accumulated savings fueled an economic surge. Manufacturers retooled for peacetime production, veterans bought homes in new suburbs with low-interest GI Bill loans, and millions attended college or vocational programs under the GI Bill— roughly eight million veterans in all—expanding the skilled workforce and the middle class.

Productivity soared across all sectors, and for a time its benefits were broadly shared. Union membership peaked in the 1950s at about 35% of the workforce, helping secure higher wages, pensions, and health benefits, especially in manufacturing. These gains lifted many working families into the middle class. White-collar and government jobs also expanded as demand rose for clerical, administrative, educational, and public-sector workers, many of them women, offering stable employment with benefits and pensions.

Government policy reinforced these trends. The federal government invested heavily in highways, education, and research institutions. It launched the National Science Foundation in 1950 and both the Defense Advanced Research Products Administration (DARPA) and NASA in 1958. State and local governments likewise poured money into schools, infrastructure, and universities. Marginal income tax rates remained very high—up to 90% under Eisenhower—helping to pay down wartime debt and finance public investment.[7]

The US also enjoyed a unique global position after World War II. Its industrial base was intact while much of Europe and Asia lay in ruins, and in 1945 the United States accounted for roughly half of the world's industrial output.

This virtuous cycle—productivity growth driving wage growth, fueling demand and still more productivity—continued until the mid-1970s. After that, the relationship changed, as shown in Figure 4 below.

....

7 Marginal tax rates are the tax amount paid on increasing increments of income. Everybody pays the same amount, say 10%, on the first $30,000. For income between say $30,000 and $50,000 the rate might be 20%. For people with very high incomes, the last "income bracket" might be very high, say over $10,000,000 and the "marginal tax rate" might be, say, 70% on that, but only on that increment.

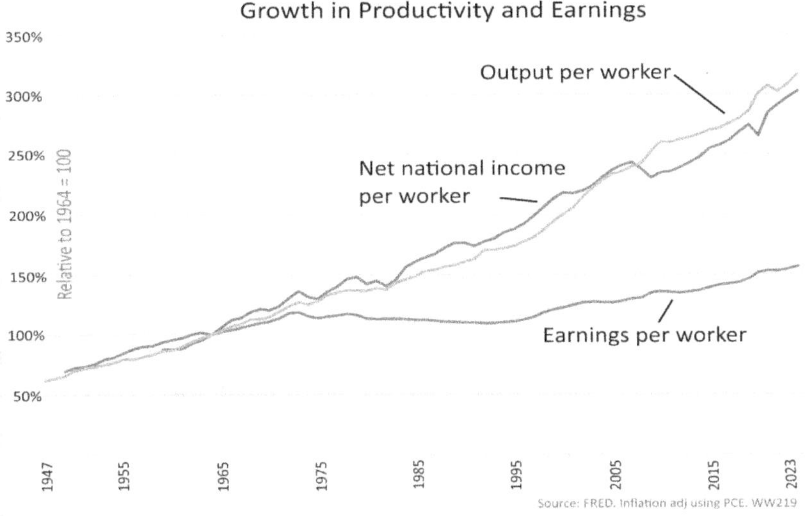

Figure 4. National Income vs Wages vs Productivity. This chart shows growth relative to the level in 1964. Growth in output kept on unabated but growth in wages did not.

We can see that productivity (output per hour worked) kept climbing, but average hourly earnings of nonsupervisory workers stagnated. Net income per worker shows the path incomes could have followed if the postwar distribution of gains had persisted. All values are adjusted for inflation.

Why did this divergence occur starting in the early 1970s?

Productivity in manufacturing continued to rise, but as firms became more efficient, they required fewer workers. Competitive pressures meant that productivity gains showed up more in lower prices than in higher wages. Lower prices are a form of higher real income— your income goes further if prices are lower—but the effect was uneven: productivity growth slowed in the expanding service sector, where most Americans now worked.

Union membership declined alongside shrinking manufacturing employment. Global trade expanded, immigration increased, tax rates were sharply reduced, and the national debt grew. The population aged, healthcare costs soared, and corporate profits rose. As shown in Figure 3, pre-tax income shares once again became more unequal. We will sort out the evidence on these factors in Chapter 2, but before we do, let's look at how government income transfers—such as Social Security, Medicare, and the Earned Income Tax Credit— affect the distribution of income.

INCOME TRANSFERS SLIGHTLY REDUCE INEQUALITY

In the introduction I mentioned that government transfers are *not* government consumption; the money is spent by, or on behalf of, the recipient. A retiree spends their Social Security check any way they want, and a Medicare or Medicaid recipient buys medical care with those transfers. A thought experiment makes this clear: suppose taxes were 100% but that government immediately turned around and gave all the money back. In this case income transfers are 100% of government spending but there is no change whatever in the economy. Transferring money does not increase or decrease national income, it just spreads it around differently. Like Robin Hood.

Figure 5 below shows US income and the federal budget for 2023. Transfers are the light boxes on the federal budget outlays line. That is how much we transfer for Social Security, Medicare, Medicaid, and programs to support the low-income households and veterans. Interest on the huge national debt is the last box on that line. That is a transfer from taxpayers to the holders of US debt. The two dark boxes on the federal budget line are "discretionary spending": defense is about half of that, and all other federal spending is the second dark box. Finally, the middle bar shows how we paid for the transfers and spending. The dark part of the bar is income taxes and contributions towards the social programs (Social Security and Medicare taxes), and the light part is borrowing. Borrowing amounts to transferring money from future earnings (and workers) to meet today's needs.

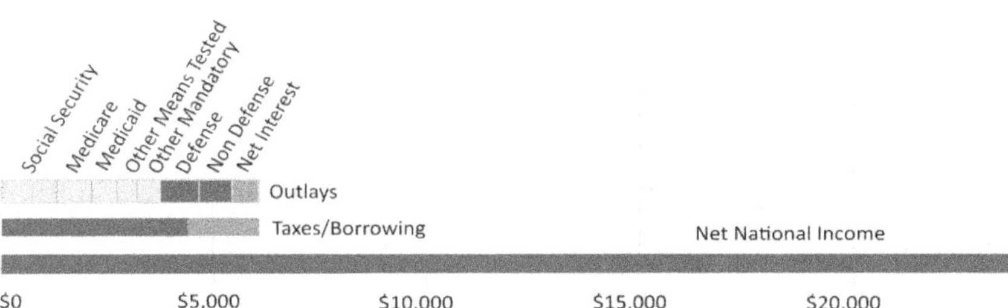

Figure 5. US National Income and Federal Budget

It is hard to look at this chart and conclude that transfers are straining our economy. But even these comparatively small transfers make a huge difference in the lives of many. Social Security doesn't just go to the needy, but it is estimated that without Social Security nearly 40% of those over the age of 65, working or not, would be below the official poverty line. With Social Security, only 10% are in official poverty.[8] Medicare and Medicaid are not paid directly to recipients so most "after taxes and transfers" statistics don't count these transfers as income, but these programs also have a major impact in people's lives. As in the case of Social Security, Medicare is not "means-tested," meaning you get this regardless of how high or low your income. The two other light outlays boxes include veterans benefits, means-tested antipoverty programs such as "food stamps," now called the Supplemental Nutrition Assistance Program, or SNAP, and the Earned Income Tax Credit. Amazing as it may seem, that little "other means-tested" box contains all of what most people call "welfare" and most of it is a small supplement to earned wages. Means-tested cash transfers, primarily the Earned Income Tax Credit (EITC) and SNAP, are about 2% of national income.[9] We'll look at these programs in more detail later.

....

8 https://www.cbpp.org/research/social-security/social-security-lifts-more-people-above-the-poverty-line-than-any-other#:~:text=Most%20people%20aged%2065%20and,benefits%2C%20only%2010.1%20percent%20do. Many feel that the official poverty line is too low.

9 https://www.cbo.gov/publication/59728 Makes "tithing" look generous!

Altogether, the effect of taxes and transfers, federal, state and local, is to increase the share of disposable national income going to the bottom half of the population back up to 20%.

Figure 5 makes it clear that we could raise taxes enough to cover the $1.7 trillion we borrowed in 2023 and that it is impossible to cut that much from discretionary spending. Instead, taxes continue to be cut, shifting income back up towards the top from the bottom. As I write this, the current administration plans to cut $800 billion from transfer programs, increase borrowing and the national debt by $5 trillion, and hand out an additional $5.4 trillion tax cut. If you are young, be aware that you will inherit this ever-increasing debt. As I will show later, we could easily eliminate borrowing without raising taxes on household incomes below around $300,000.

WORKING BUT POOR

While we all have some idea how the rich live from TV shows, there is a vast pool of people in the US barely making ends meet, despite working full time. In 2019, 53 million people, or 44% of America's workers, were low wage, with median hourly wages of $10.22 and median annual earnings of $17,950. Low-wage workers switch jobs frequently but mostly churn within a set of low-wage occupations. Almost 40% of Americans can't afford an expense of over $400 without borrowing. About two-thirds of Americans don't have a college degree.[10]

As these statistics suggest, economic mobility is low for people born into low-income families. Economic mobility is the likelihood that you will rise or fall in the income rankings. Compared to other wealthy countries, chances for upward mobility are good for the middle class in the US but poor for people born into families towards the lower end of the income scale. Mobility is also low for those born into rich families: They tend to stay rich. One result has been a shrinking of the middle class. Pew research says that the middle class has shrunk from just over 60% of adults in 1971 to about

---

10 https://www.brookings.edu/articles/meet-the-low-wage-workforce/ 2019

half in 2021, with both the upper- and lower-income groups increasing in size. In their analysis, about 30% of US adults are lower income while 21% are upper income, which implies again that household income distribution has become more unequal.

Not all low-wage workers are in low-income households: Students work, and many low-wage workers have spouses who make more. But 27 million low-wage workers are either the only earners in their household or are in households where all the other earners are low-wage.

What occupations employ many low-wage workers? In the service sector, fast food workers, restaurant servers and bussers, hotel housekeepers, janitors and cleaning staff, cashiers, shelf stockers, store clerks and salespeople, and home health aides are often low-wage. Farmworkers, landscapers, meatpacking and poultry workers have low wages. Childcare workers, teacher's aides, and paraprofessionals in schools are low-wage. In transportation, rideshare drivers, food delivery workers (especially in gig-economy settings), and warehouse pickers and packers are typically low-wage. Other occupations with low pay include laundry workers, parking lot attendants, and security guards. These examples pay near or below the federal poverty threshold of about $15/hour for a full-time worker, and there is little chance for advancement. If you're better off, you may not realize how many of the people you interact with every day are just getting by, often with help from such programs as SNAP, Section 8 housing assistance, and of course Medicaid. A 2020 study found that Walmart and McDonald's are among the top employers of individuals relying on food stamps (SNAP) and Medicaid to make ends meet and stay insured. These jobs offer little in the way of advancement, and the means-tested social programs and Earned Income Tax Credit effectively reduce and, in some cases, eliminate the financial benefit of increased wages, a subject we'll look at in more detail later. Overall, a shocking 30% of Americans are poor or near poor.

WEALTH INEQUALITY IS EXTREME

Income is how much you earn in a year. Wealth measures how much you own. Wealth concentration in the US is extreme. Currently it really is true that three men have more wealth than half of all Americans put together. In Figure 6 we see that one-third of US wealth is held by the top 1% and another one-third is held by the rest of the top tenth. In other words, the top 10% of US households hold about two-thirds of all wealth. The middle class below the top 10% but above 50% holds the final third, mostly through equity in their homes. And the lower half of Americans have next to no wealth at all. Figure 7 shows that the average wealth of the top 1% of households is nearly $40,000,000, totaling $52 trillion.

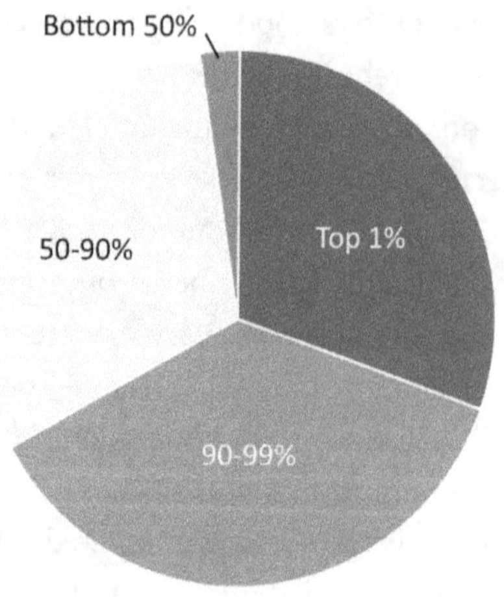

Figure 6. Wealth Shares. The top 1% own one third of the wealth, the bottom 50% almost none. Source: FED.

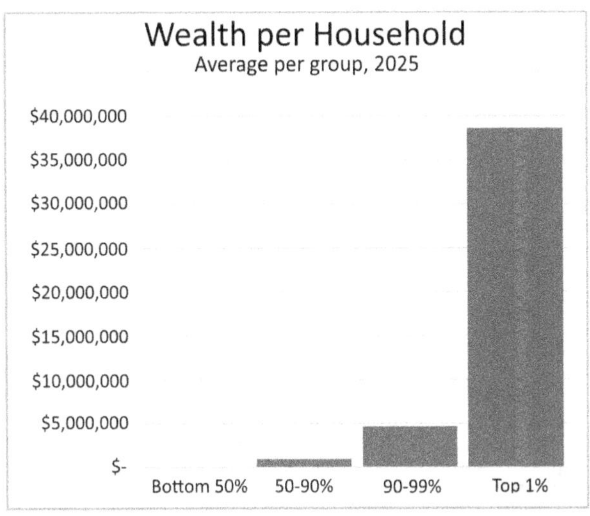

Figure 7. Average Wealth per Income Group. The top 1% has an average wealth of $40 million. Source: FED.

In the US, wealth concentration also went through "the Great Compression" during and after the Great Depression and the World Wars until about 1980. This drop in wealth inequality was thanks to the rapid expansion of home ownership by the middle class, financed by the GI Bill and booming economy, and by the widespread adoption of pension plans by employers. In other words, it wasn't that the wealth of the rich declined, it was rather that the middle class accumulated wealth at an even faster rate. As in the case of income, that trend reversed in the US around the time of Reagan's election in1980, and for similar reasons to the rise of income inequality. It is interesting to note that wealth inequality in 1914 was higher in western Europe than in the US but fell further due to the wartime destruction of capital and, after the wars, progressive economic policies as in the US. But European countries continued to expand and maintain progressive policies and taxation, so that wealth inequality has declined further there and, as shown in Figure 8, hasn't risen again the way it has in the US.

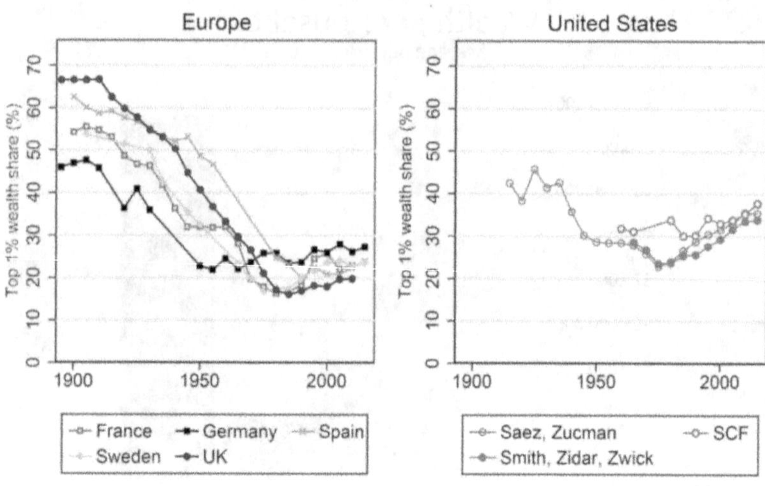

Figure 8. Top 1% Wealth Share in Europe and the US. Source: Waldenström, Daniel. 2024[11]

The influence of such a staggering concentration of wealth is easy to understand. Politics and public discussion and opinions are dominated by monied interests in a way that they weren't back in the days of the robber barons and the muckraking newspapers. There were thousands of them back then. Today US newspapers and TV stations are largely owned by a few massive media conglomerates like Comcast (NBCUniversal), Disney (ABC), Paramount Global (CBS), Fox Corp, and Hearst, alongside large chains like Gannett, Tribune/Media News Group, and Nexstar for local TV, often with significant control by private equity/hedge funds. As we'll see later, the rich have used this dominance to largely control a narrative and politics favorable to their interests. Such concentration of wealth is extremely unhealthy for a democracy and the interests of the broad population.

11 Waldenström, Daniel. 2024. "A New History of Wealth Inequality in the West." CEPR. November 2024. https://cepr.org/voxeu/columns/new-history-wealth-inequality-west.

2

WHY ARE INCOME AND WEALTH INEQUALITY GROWING? THE ECONOMICS VIEW

In Chapter 1, we saw that productivity growth has made the US and other first world countries rich, but that in the US, income and wealth distribution is highly skewed and has become more so since Reagan's time. Productivity gains have continuously reduced the need for general labor, and basic economics tells us that reducing demand for anything without reducing its supply will lead to lower prices.[12] Falling demand for general labor, or an increase in the supply of general labor, will cause wages to stagnate. The case for increased productivity putting downward pressure on the demand for general labor in agriculture and manufacturing is clear: It simply takes far fewer workers to grow food or manufacture goods now thanks to the use of machinery and automation. Despite that, many across the political spectrum allege that trade has helped "hollow out" US manufacturing, leading to the loss of "good-paying manufacturing jobs" for general labor. And immigrants are blamed for increasing the supply of general labor, competing for jobs and so lowering wages. How important are these other factors by comparison with automation and productivity growth?

In addition to these labor demand and supply factors, union membership has declined, progressive taxation has essentially been eliminated, CEO pay has mushroomed, and corporate profits have swelled. Below we'll look at the relative impact of each of these factors on the stagnation of wages for most people and the ballooning of income and wealth at the top.

DEINDUSTRIALIZATION AND TRADE

Manufacturing employed about one-third of workers in the early 1950s, but it employs less than 10% of workers now. Those jobs didn't require extensive training but could support a middle-class lifestyle. The decline of factory jobs, like the earlier shift from agricultural employment, led to painful job dislocations and a surplus of general labor as workers had to find other work.

....

12 Usually, "general labor" means blue-collar physical labor. But in this book I use the term to mean any work that doesn't require extensive training. Jobs in fast food or data entry are also "general labor" by this definition.

Manufacturing has declined as fraction of employment in all the rich countries. Even in China it has fallen slightly over the last decade. Figure 9 below shows the decline in manufacturing employment for several rich countries along with the dates when NAFTA was signed and China was admitted into the World Trade Organization. As you can see, employment in manufacturing declined in all these countries—even in Germany, which ran, and still runs, a huge trade surplus. The US ran a trade surplus until 1970 and comparatively small trade deficits until the late 1990s, so the decline in manufacturing employment as a percentage of total employment is clearly not due to trade in that part of the chart.

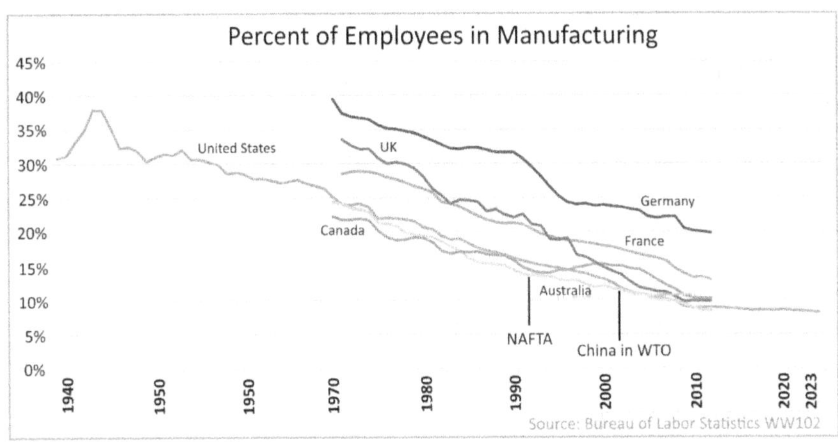

Figure 9. Manufacturing Employment as a Percent of Total Employment.

In the US, real output per manufacturing worker has risen more than threefold since 1970: That is, it now takes one worker to produce as much stuff as three workers in 1970. Figure 10 below is an example of a modern automated car plant, there's not a human in sight. This one is in the US, but it could be anywhere in the world, Chinese automobile plants are among the most highly automated on earth. With declining employment in agriculture and manufacturing, four-fifths of US workers now work in what are called services, where productivity growth has been somewhat slower. That may change with the advent of AI.

Figure 10. Plant Automation.

Automation and other productivity enhancements are a major factor in declining employment in manufacturing. But international trade has increased enormously—surely that too is a factor in reducing employment in manufacturing? The answer is yes; it has been a factor in the decline. As trade increased worldwide, "labor intensive" factory work such as making clothes moved to developing countries where labor is even more abundant and cheap. That displaced clothing workers in the US and other high-wage countries. But clothing workers weren't very well paid in the US in any case. During the early 1970s, employees at Farah Manufacturing Company—a major clothing producer—were reported to earn approximately $1.60 per hour, which was the federal minimum wage at the time. This wage equated to about $69 per week, or roughly $3,588 annually, placing many of these manufacturing workers near or below the poverty line for a family of four during that period.[13] A couple of things happened when the flow of cheap

....

13 These numbers are for the Texas. Pay was modest but higher in other locations. See DOYLE, PHILIP M. "WAGES IN DRESS MANUFACTURING VARY WIDELY BY AREA." Monthly Labor Review 96, no. 3 (1973): 57–62.

imported clothes ramped up: First, US clothing workers were displaced and had to find other work, and second, the price of clothing fell drastically. Now the clothing workers could hardly have taken jobs offering wages any lower than they'd been earning, so if they found new jobs, they didn't lose much economically. On the other hand, the drastically lower cost of clothes effectively gave everyone in the US a pay raise. In 1960, an average American household spent over 10% of its income on clothing and shoes—equivalent to roughly $5,600 today. The average person bought fewer than 25 garments each year. And about 95% of those clothes were made in the United States. By 2013, the average American household spent less than 3.5% of its budget on clothing and shoes—under $2,500 today—to buy close to 70 pieces of clothing per person. About 2% of that was made in the US. The savings of over $3,000 per household come to $390 *billion per year*—way more than the income losses of clothing workers who would have found other work in any case.[14]

That is the general story of trade: It lowers costs, but *new* trade competition can cause employment dislocations. Trade is an important aspect of our economy, and it's helpful to have a basic understanding of trading economics. To start with, there are only two reasons to buy from another state or country: The item is cheaper, or you can't make it locally. Think of clothing and bananas: We buy clothing from abroad because it's cheaper, and we buy bananas from abroad because we can't grow them here. Trade always does one of these two things: It lowers prices, or it makes new goods available. Trade has two sides: Both parties must be made better off by a trade, at least in the short run, or it won't happen. For both parties to be better off, every country tends to make and export what they are "best" at. In economics this is called "comparative advantage." If Vietnam has low-cost labor, then they will have an advantage in producing clothing that is labor-intensive, compared to a country such as Germany or the US. The US exports agricultural products, machinery, mechanical appliances, chemicals, plastics, rubber, and leather goods to Vietnam. It has a comparative

---

14 These numbers come from "Why America Stopped Making Its Own Clothes" by Stephanie Vatz May 24, 2013, on WQED. https://www.kqed.org/lowdown/7939/madeinamerica . Updated to 2025 dollars. Note that since clothing workers made essentially minimum wage, switching to other jobs did not result in major income loss. Overall levels of employment remained high.

advantage in producing these products. Since comparative advantage lines up with productivity and income, this trade means that *average* per capita income rises in both countries. Think of it this way: If the US didn't buy clothing from Vietnam, workers here would have to make the clothing, which is a low-productivity business compared to producing the products we sell to Vietnam. We'd end up making more low-productivity, low-income stuff and less high-productivity, high-income stuff, making us poorer overall. I should note that unemployment remained relatively low over the period, so, as in the case of clothing workers, trade didn't lead to job losses but rather displacement of workers from one type of job to another.

Before we can quantify the effect of trade on the US, we need to consider one more wrinkle: what happens when there is a trade "shock." When trade patterns have been stable for some time, an equilibrium is formed. Let's say that year after year we buy clothing from Vietnam, and they buy the stuff we listed above from us. Trade is balanced, tariffs are stable, and companies can make long-run investments. Employment is stable too. There are few people employed in clothing manufacturing in the US, but many people are employed in the relatively more productive, higher income US industries that export to Vietnam.

What happens when there is a drastic change in trade? That can happen because tariffs are changed (either reduced or increased), or because a large developing country like China grows its manufacturing sector quickly as a largely rural agrarian population moves to cities, or because shipping costs are drastically lowered. In fact, all these factors played a part in the greatly expanded trade between China and the US and other rich countries starting around the turn of the twenty-first century, reaching a plateau of 2.4% of GDP in the US around 2010, and then declining after 2018[15]. This has been referred to by economists as the "China Shock." In Figure 9, the China Shock starts around the time of China's acceptance into the World Trade Organization and clearly occurs well after most of the drop in manufacturing employment in the US. In fact, manufacturing employment

....

15 See https://fred.stlouisfed.org/series/IMPCH# If one divides by GDP, the trend is even clearer

largely stabilized in the US after 2010. Nonetheless, the "shock" of greatly expanded China trade did cause many factories to close in the US, and many people lost their jobs. Between 2001 and 2011, US apparel manufacturing employment fell by about 50% as thousands of textile mills closed, especially in the Southeast US (North Carolina, South Carolina, Georgia). California and Texas lost consumer electronics manufacturing jobs. The Midwest and Rust Belt states lost automotive component manufacturing jobs. Even the Northeast lost high-tech manufacturing jobs as Chinese firms expanded their capabilities. These manufacturing job losses depressed local economies with heavy concentrations of the affected industry. Workers who lost their jobs, especially those who didn't move away, often took jobs paying less in the service economy.

We now have the basic economic background to try to sort out the effects of trade, and the trade deficit, on employment and income in the US. How in particular do we reconcile the economists' conviction that trade increases productivity and raises incomes, mostly through lower prices, with the effects just noted of the trade shock? Two things must be kept in mind. First, after a trade shock, some industries grow as others decline, and eventually a new dynamic equilibrium is reached. Greenville, South Carolina, a place I'm familiar with, lost most of its textile mills between the late 1970s and the 1990s, long before the China Shock. Greenville is now a major hub for advanced manufacturing including automotive, aerospace, materials, healthcare, and life sciences. Michelin and BMW have factories nearby. The economy is booming, but inequality and poverty are close to US averages. There are fewer millwork-type jobs available for general labor, but more jobs in advanced manufacturing. Second, while some industries and workers suffer as plants close, trade lowers prices, often dramatically, as we saw in the case of clothing. Lower prices are the same as increased income. In statistics adjusted for inflation, lower prices show up as wage increases, even when the dollar amount of wages doesn't change.

Trade, in short, raises the country's overall productivity and income and lowers prices. Changes in trade patterns create winners and losers, but after industry adjusts, there are fewer dislocations.

The chart below shows US imports and exports as a percentage of GDP. In 2023 our imports were $3.8 trillion and our exports $3 trillion. As imports have risen, so have exports. Some industries have contracted while others have grown.

Figure 11. US Imports and Exports, Percent of GDP.

It is estimated that exports directly and indirectly support about 10.2 million jobs, or 7% of total US employment.[16] Export-related jobs such as high tech and financial services pay more than average wages.[17] About a trillion dollars of our exports are now in services, including financial and legal services and domestic tourism. A new trade shock, such as large changes in tariffs, would have large employment consequences.

On the flip side, the net benefits of imports to the US economy were estimated in the range of $1,600 to over $6,000 *per family per year*.[18] That would be the cost to the average family if everything we buy from overseas was instead made here. Of course, getting back to that point would be hell.

....

16 https://www.trade.gov/feature-article/otea-publications#:~:text=In%202022%2C%20it%20is%20estimated,to%20have%20
supported%204%2C100%20jobs.

17 https://ustr.gov/archive/Benefits_of_Trade/States/Section_Index.html

18 See How Large Are the US Economy's Gains from Trade? | NBER . The family calculation is based on the range of 2% to 8% of GDP and 2023 GDP.

I've digressed from the topic of the quantifying the role of trade in reducing manufacturing employment in the US. As trade has grown, labor-intensive (low-paying, high-employment) manufacturing has declined in the US, while employment in high-value (high-pay, lower-employment) manufacturing and services for export has increased. On net there are fewer manufacturing jobs now in the US than there would be without trade, even if there were no trade deficit. It is estimated that the "China Shock" resulted in the loss of about 2.4 million manufacturing jobs between 1990 and 2007, or 21% of the manufacturing job loss over the period.[19] That means that around 80% of the decline was due to other factors, mainly productivity growth through automation. Now that the economy has adjusted, very few additional jobs losses are due to trade.

There is one aspect of trade that does not make us richer: the trade deficit. In the chart above (Figure 11) you can see that we import more than we export. In dollar terms, the difference was around $800 billion in 2023. The trade deficit essentially lets us buy an excess of foreign goods today by borrowing money and by selling assets. We borrow money from foreigners by selling them treasury bonds to finance our national debt, and we sell them assets in the form of US companies and stock. It is beyond the scope of this discussion to say whether and how to fix the trade deficit (we should); what we're interested in is whether reducing the trade deficit would bring back manufacturing jobs.[20] Unfortunately, the answer to that question depends on how one goes about deficit reduction. Effectively devaluing the dollar against other currencies (see footnote 20) would make US-produced goods and services cheaper and foreign goods and services more expensive, reducing or even closing the deficit. Since we mostly buy manufactured goods, rather than services, from overseas, that would increase manufacturing employment, but only modestly. Estimates run in the range of one to two million manufacturing jobs, which one must stack up against approximately 33 million additional jobs required to bring us back to the employment share

19 David H. Autor, David Dorn, and Gordon H. Hanson, 2013, "The China Syndrome: Local Labor Market Effects of Import Competition in the United States," The *American Economic Review* 103 (6): 2121–68.

20 Yes, we should reduce the trade deficit, and no broad tariffs aren't the way to do it. See this article for some ideas: https://www.piie.com/blogs/trade-and-investment policy watch/three-ways-reduce-trade-deficit

of 1950. Unemployment at the end of 2024 was at a 50-year low, so creating new jobs, factory or otherwise, would mean people switching from one job to another rather than increasing employment. The pay for these jobs, as always, would be determined by the supply and demand of the types of labor needed.

To summarize, deindustrialization, the long-term loss of manufacturing jobs in the US and other rich countries, is mostly due to the fact that more stuff can be made with less labor because of automation and more machines. Trade has also reduced employment in manufacturing, but with major benefits such as lower prices. Both higher productivity and trade increase *overall* real national income. The trade deficit, if eliminated or reduced, would modestly increase manufacturing employment. Even in the complete absence of trade, deindustrialization is here to stay. Nobody seems to find it a problem that agriculture only employs 1% of the workforce to grow all the food we need, although that has severely reduced agricultural employment. The same thing has happened in manufacturing. We are not going back to 1820 in agriculture or 1950 in manufacturing, and that's a good thing. But in both cases the result has been the displacement of general labor from manufacturing or agricultural jobs to service jobs.

IMMIGRATION'S EFFECT ON EMPLOYMENT AND WAGES

Another common perception is that immigration has put competitive pressure on the wages of general labor. This contention is as old as immigration itself and has been levied against every wave of immigrants into the US. Immigrants, now and in prior times, contend for jobs in construction, agriculture, meatpacking, healthcare, domestic work, hospitality, and yes, manufacturing. In some of these occupations, recent immigrants are currently essential because it would require much higher wages to entice workers who have been in the country longer regardless of whether they are native born or not. Fourteen percent of Americans are immigrants, but two-thirds of US farmworkers are foreign-born. Indeed, almost half of all farmworkers are undocumented immigrants. About half of all meatpackers are foreign-born and a substantial percent undocumented. Forty percent of home health aides are immigrants and a quarter or more of construction workers are undocumented immigrants. At the other extreme of the pay scale, a quarter of doctors and surgeons are foreign-born.

Immigrants have been used to weaken or break unions. An example is provided by the meatpacking industry in the US. More than a century ago, Sinclair Lewis wrote *The Jungle* about the Chicago meatpacking industry, which at that time was dangerous and dirty and largely conducted by immigrants from Europe. Over time, the meatpackers unionized and, as noted by author Eric Schlosser, "by the early 1970s, a job at a meatpacking plant offered stable employment, high wages, good benefits, and the promise of a middle-class life."[21] Eric goes on the describe what happened next:

> As I described in my book *Fast Food Nation*, published in 2001, the largest companies in the beef industry had recruited immigrants in Mexico, brought them to the meatpacking communities of the American West and Midwest, and used them during the Ronald Reagan era to break unions. Wages were soon cut by as much as 50%. Line speeds were increased, government oversight was reduced, and injured workers were once again forced to remain on the job or get fired.

The same thing happened in poultry processing. In December 2001, *The New York Times* reported:

> The government charged the company (Tyson Foods Inc.) and six of its employees with conspiring to transport illegal immigrants across the Mexican border and help them get counterfeit work papers for jobs at more than a dozen Tyson poultry plants. The indictment said that, to meet production and profit goals, Tyson officials would contact local smugglers near its plants to get more workers.[22]

---

21 Schlosser, Eric. 2019. "Why It's Immigrants Who Pack Your Meat." The Atlantic, August 16, 2019. https://www.theatlantic.com/ideas/archive/2019/08/trumps-invasion-was-a-corporate-recruitment-drive/596230/.

22 Barboza, David. 2001. "Meatpackers' Profits Hinge on Pool of Immigrant Labor." The New York Times, December 21, 2001. https://www.nytimes.com/2001/12/21/us/meatpackers-profits-hinge-on-pool-of-immigrant-labor.html.

Clearly the domestic workers in the unionized meatpacking industry were hurt by this exploitation of immigrants.

But there is a flip side to the story of even low-skilled immigrants. The American Farm Bureau Federation calls for immigration reform to *increase* the number of farmworkers, noting that "the impacts of an enforcement only approach to immigration would be detrimental to the agricultural industry. If agriculture were to lose access to all undocumented workers, agricultural output would fall by $30 to $60 billion... . Many migrants who begin their careers as farm laborers move onto other sectors of the economy or less demanding positions after several years. This progression leads to farmers often being the first to bear the negative economic impacts of decreased border crossings and migrant labor shortages.[23] Maybe that's the reason Trump, despite all the noise, deported fewer undocumented migrants during his first term than Obama had in the prior four years.

As with productivity and trade, while some native workers are negatively affected by the inflow of migrants, most of us benefit. The price of meat and agricultural products is much lower than it would be in the absence of migrants, as are the costs for home health aides, domestic and hospitality workers, and other goods and services where migrants, especially undocumented ones, make up a significant share of the workforce.

A couple of migrant-related facts are worth noting. The native birth rate in all rich countries is below what is called the replacement rate of 2.1 children per woman. That means that the population size would fall in the absence of migration. Worse, the population is aging, leaving fewer younger workers to support older retired people. Immigrants tend to be young, which helps keep the ratio of those working to those receiving retirement benefits better balanced. Recent immigrants put a strain on local resources and are a net cost to local and state governments. The children of immigrants, however, are above average in their net positive contribution to government revenue

....

23 "Agriculture Labor Reform." n.d. American Farm Bureau Federation. Accessed January 29, 2023. https://www.fb.org/issue/labor/agriculture-labor-reform.

at all levels.[24] In other words, they pay more in state, local, and federal taxes than they cost in services and benefits. Immigrant families are also sources of demand as well as labor, so they grow the overall economy. After the first generation, they become "like everybody else" in economic terms.

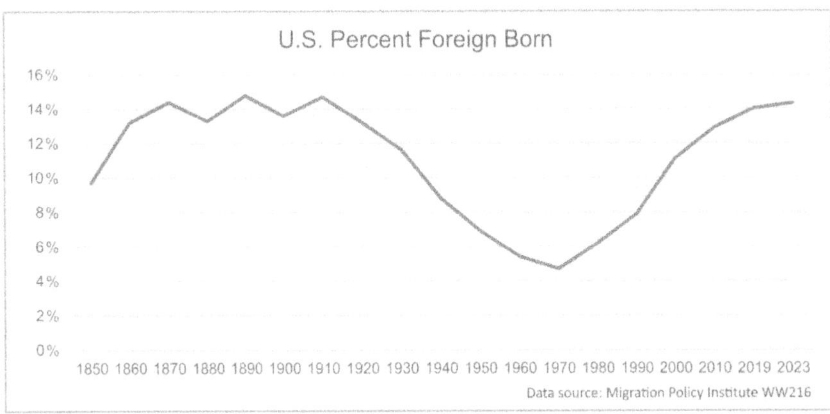

Figure 12. Percentage of the US Population That Is Foreign-Born.

The United States hosts the largest number of migrants in the world, about 47.8 million in 2023, or about 14.3% of the population, but several wealthy countries, such as Canada, Australia, and Germany host more migrants as a percentage of their populations. Of the 47.8 million foreign-born, roughly 11 million (23%) are thought to be undocumented.

In 1965 Congress passed the Immigration and Nationality Act (aka the Hart-Celler Act), which scrapped the former country-based quotas that favored northern and western European immigrants. The bill was passed with bipartisan support from Republicans and Northern Democrats and opposed by Southern Democrats, racist in that era, who wanted to maintain a white-majority racial order. In the chart above you can see that the number of foreign-born in the US started climbing after that reform.

24 National Academies of Sciences, Engineering, and Medicine, Division of Behavioral and Social Sciences and Education, Committee on National Statistics, and Panel on the Economic and Fiscal Consequences of Immigration, 2017, *The Economic and Fiscal Consequences of Immigration*. National Academies Press, page 12.

The Hart-Celler Act set the rules for legal immigration still enforced today. It applied a system of preferences for family reunification (75%), skilled employment (20%), and refugees (5%) and for the first time capped immigration from within the Americas.[25] Under Hart-Celler there are regional caps, but none for immediate relatives. Since the early 1990s legal immigration into the country has averaged around one million per year, under all presidents including during Trump's first term. There was a large temporary spike after amnesty was granted to undocumented migrants by the immigration reform bill signed by Reagan in 1986. That bill also introduced penalties for businesses that knowingly hired undocumented migrants but otherwise didn't change the immigration rules. In 1996, under Clinton, an immigration bill was passed that tightened enforcement, expanded deportation authority, expanded immigration detention, and limited appeals. That also did not change the basic rules about who was legally entitled to immigrate. Attempts to reform immigration since that time have failed, not surprisingly given that both business and agriculture are strongly pro-immigration.

Economists who study immigration generally agree that immigration has not negatively affected overall employment levels. No surprise there since we were pretty much at full employment in late 2024. They also agree that immigration has increased overall GDP. Again, no surprise, as the population grows, so does GDP. There is no consensus on whether immigrants increase GDP per capita, but mostly because if there is an effect it is way too small to stand out. States with higher immigrant percentages have higher state GDP per capita, but it is impossible to tell whether one causes the other or vice versa. Finally, regarding impact on wages, a paper reviewing the studies concluded:

> When measured over a period of more than 10 years, the impact of immigration on the wages of natives overall is very small. However, estimates for subgroups span a comparatively wider range, indicating a revised and somewhat more detailed understanding of the wage impact of immigration since the 1990s. To the extent that negative wage effects are found, prior

25 See "Timeline," 2018, Immigration History, The University of Texas at Austin Department of History. February 27, 2018. https://immigrationhistory.org/timeline/. Also https://en.wikipedia.org/wiki/Immigration_and_Nationality_Act_of_1965.

immigrants — who are often the closest substitutes for new immigrants — are most likely to experience them, followed by native-born high school dropouts, who share job qualifications similar to the large share of low-skilled [fewer years of school] workers among immigrants to the United States. 26

In short, immigration, like trade, lowers prices for the public on agriculture and meatpacking products and many services, but negatively affects the wages of earlier migrants and native-born workers in general labor occupations, at least where anyone else is willing to work those jobs. By far the bulk of immigrants come here legally. In fiscal year 2018 a total of 1,096,611 new lawful permanent residents were admitted (91,000 per month). The published number for the first quarter of fiscal year 2025, when 116,666 lawful permanent residents were accepted per month.[27] Given the support for immigration by the US Chamber of Commerce and big farming organizations, it is very unlikely that there will be any move in Congress or by the current administration to change *legal* immigration rules.

THE "REAGAN REVOLUTION"

Automation, trade, and immigration have all contributed to a continuing softness in the market for general labor, but it took some time for that to affect the distribution of national income. There was also a cultural change carefully nurtured by monied interests and reflected in politics, which I will discuss later.

In the section on the fall and rise of inequality, we saw that income inequality, which had fallen after World War II, started rising again after Reagan's election in 1980. We also saw that total national income per person kept right on rising uninterrupted. What changed was that an increasing share of income went to the top 10% again. Even the middle-class share of income fell. Figure 13 illustrates the change.

....

26 National Academies of Science, 2017, p. 5.

27 See https://ohss.dhs.gov/topics/immigration/legal-immigration-and-adjustment-status-report

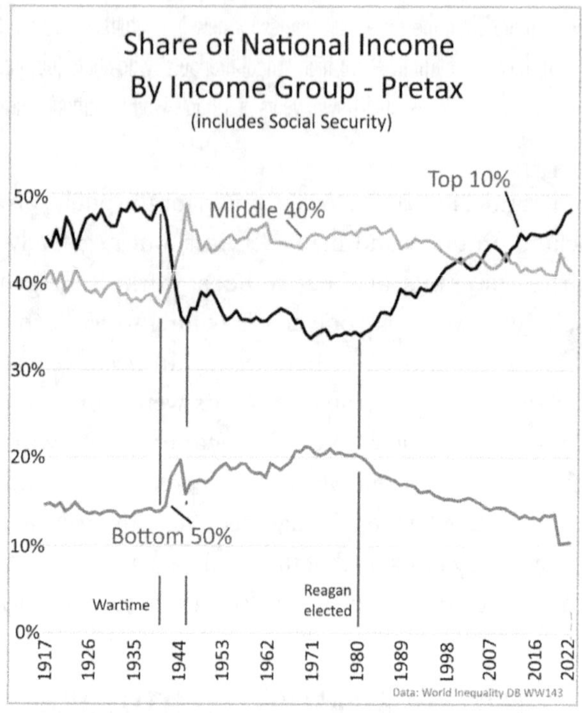

Figure 13. Distribution of National Income.

This is income pretax and -transfers, so the trend is not directly due to Reagan's famous "trickle down" tax cuts for the wealthy, although those cuts made post-tax inequality worse. The increasing 10% share and declining 50% share continued under presidents and congresses of both parties. What changed were attempts to address inequality through various transfer programs, regulations, and industrial policies. We'll look at those later too—here we're looking at the economics. In a market economy, wages, like prices, are determined by supply and demand for any specific type of labor. We've seen that enormous productivity growth in manufacturing, like prior growth in agriculture, reduced the demand for general labor, with trade and immigration contributing, but to a much lesser extent. The weak labor market in turn weakened the bargaining power of labor unions. Unions played a key role in boosting worker pay and improving working conditions in the first half of the twentieth century, but by the time Reagan was elected unions were in decline along with manufacturing employment.

The air traffic controllers' strike of 1981 was a watershed moment for unions. The controllers, like other federal employees, were barred from striking, but in 1980 their union, PATCO, had used sick-outs and work slowdowns to call attention to poor working conditions and other grievances. The relationship between the Carter administration's FAA and the air traffic controllers was strained as a result. During his presidential campaign, candidate Reagan wrote to the president of PATCO declaring support for the union's demands, and PATCO, along with the Teamsters and the Air Line Pilots Association, supported his candidacy instead of Carter's.

Once elected, Reagan had the same problems as Carter in dealing with the union. PATCO called for a 32-hour work week, a $10,000 pay increase for all air traffic controllers, and a better benefits package for retirement. The FAA responded with a relatively generous pay offer that did not include a shorter work week, but the union rejected the offer and instead initiated an illegal strike. In the end, Reagan fired the controllers who did not return to work, and the FAA began replacing them with a combination of about 3,000 supervisors, 2,000 non-striking air traffic controllers, and 900 military controllers. According to Paul Volker, the Federal Reserve chair, during this period, Reagan mostly followed contingency plans developed during the Carter administration.[28] The air traffic controllers were often working-class men who had achieved a middle-class suburban lifestyle without a college education; many had been trained in the military. In the aftermath of the strike, strikers who were fired mostly took lower-paying work or were forced into poverty.

The breaking of the PATCO strike demonstrated that labor unions were weak and set a precedent for simply firing and rehiring workers. Numerous corporations, including Hormel, Phelps Dodge, and International Paper, provoked legal strikes among their employees and then hired replacement

28 "Commanding Heights, Paul Volcker," PBS, accessed June 16, 2021.

workers during the strikes to force major concessions from unions.[29] The stagflation and high unemployment of the early 1980s made this especially easy. The number of major strikes declined from 235 in 1979 to 62 in 1984.[30] Three-quarters of the public viewed unions favorably in 1957; by the 1980s only half did. Many saw unions as bureaucratic, narrowly focused, sometimes corrupt, and fostering inefficiency that kept US business from being competitive. Media often amplified these perceptions. But while the shifting political winds were important, unions declined mostly because of deindustrialization. As employment shifted from heavily unionized manufacturing to less unionized services, union membership fell.

Higher levels of unemployment, weaker and fewer unions, and a changed political climate set the stage for companies to "maximize shareholder value," which for many CEOs meant maximizing short-term profits and hence stock prices and dividends. Employees were squeezed and CEO incentive pay soared. Corporate earnings rose to post–World War II levels and kept climbing. Pre-tax corporate profits were $4 trillion by the end of 2024, which was more than the pre-tax and -transfer earnings of the lower half of US households.

29 https://libraries.uta.edu/news/1981-patco-strike. Attributed to Joseph A. McCartin.
30 https://www.bls.gov/wsp/factsheets/summary-of-work-stoppages-in-the-united-states.htm.

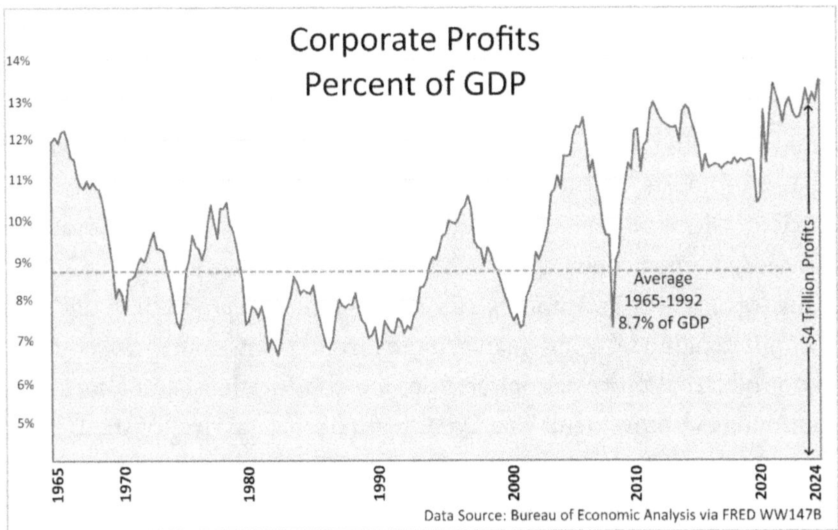

Figure 14. Corporate Profits as a Percent of GDP

During this period of rising corporate profits, labor's share of national income declined, and wage inequality increased. Labor share of national income is the fraction of the income pie going to employees, which is most of us, including salaried managers and professionals as well as production workers. The labor share of national income has declined from about 67% in 1988 to 58% in 2024, representing a fall of more than $2 trillion a year. At the same time wage inequality has also increased, meaning that many managers and professionals have seen wage gains greater than other employees. Output per worker has kept on growing but regular employees have taken home a shrinking portion of national income. Increasing output per hour is a good thing, and output kept growing driven by increasing productivity and trade.[31] But the fruits of greater productivity have not been widely shared, even when one allows for labor being replaced with capital. [32]

....

31 To calculate GDP per capita over time, output dollars have to be adjusted for inflation. Trade reduces goods prices (as does higher productivity, especially in manufacturing). This shows up as higher real GDP thus increasing calculated output per capita.

32 As capital is substituted for labor, a greater share of income must be used to compensate capital owners. Example: If you replace one worker with one machine, labor productivity goes up for the remaining workers (fewer workers, same output), but the machine cost money. For a deeper discussion of why labor share has declined see https://www.mckinsey.com/featured-insights/employment-and-growth/a-new-look-at-the-declining-labor-share-of-income-in-the-united-states which includes a review of studies.

The benefits of increased productivity *can* be shared with labor while allowing companies room to become more efficient. The United Auto Workers union demonstrated this in its dealings with the "Big 3" automakers. In the early 1980s US automakers were getting hammered by Japanese imports, which were often cheaper, better made, and more fuel-efficient. GM wanted to learn "lean manufacturing," a Toyota innovation, but needed union cooperation. With UAW agreement, a joint GM–Toyota plant was built in Freemont, California, with labor proceeding under a very different model using smaller, more flexible teams, more worker input into production processes, fewer strict job classifications, and a focus on continuous improvement. The UAW realized that survival of the US car companies required modernization and worked with management to get the best deal it could for labor without unduly hampering progress.

Then, in 2008, the financial crisis hit, and GM and Chrysler headed for bankruptcy. The UAW took over tens of billions of dollars in retiree health care liabilities, greatly improving the company's balance sheets. The union made other significant wage and benefit concessions, which together with Obama's bridge loans, helped the companies reorganize in 2009. Fast-forward to 2023. The car companies were making record profits but foresaw the need for massive investment to produce electric cars. Also, their labor costs were still higher in the northern union plants than in the non-union plants in the south. UAW was unconvinced by these management concerns and, through a rolling strike against all three companies, won concessions that gave workers a larger share of income again. Most workers in the US aren't members of a union, and not all unions are as flexible as the UAW, but this kind of adversarial-yet-strangely-cooperative relationship between labor and management works. In the end, while contentious, labor and management really do sometimes understand they are part of a "team," a term that's only an empty slogan unless the benefits of productivity are shared. Not all union GM workers may hold GM stock, but like shareholders, they benefit from the success of the company. Unfortunately, outside of government, union membership stands at only 6% of the workforce now, down from about 33% in 1954.

Up to now, we've been looking at what caused median wages to diverge from productivity, and income inequality to grow, before taxes. The "Reagan Revolution" also called for massive tax cuts, especially at the upper end of the income scale. The idea was that wealthy people can't reasonably consume all their income and if they have more after-tax income they will invest more. In turn that investment will drive productivity growth and overall national income. Higher national productivity will "trickle down" to workers as higher real wages, and the growth in income will more than compensate for the lower tax rates. Turns out this was economic fantasy, and the deficit ballooned. Reagan was forced to agree to raise taxes several times, but he retained, and in fact increased, the cuts to the highest income tax brackets. However, payroll taxes for Social Security and Medicare, which fall mostly on the middle class and poor, were increased. Overall spending was not cut, resulting in a tripling of the national debt during Reagan's presidency, a pattern that has persisted to this day.[33] As for "trickle down," as the UAW example makes clear, companies only increase worker pay if labor market conditions or law require it—that's basic market economics, not a moral failing. Unions give labor more market power, but for non-unionized workers, almost all of us now, the labor market dictates the pay and terms, especially for general labor. Certainly, individual skill, effort, and seniority will affect pay, but many general labor jobs offer little opportunity for growth, and pay scales are compressed. We've seen that a large fraction of US workers churn through general labor jobs and that income mobility within that group is low. Workers in the middle class have a better chance of upward mobility, but the middle-class portion of national income has also declined as the top 10% eats up most of the gains.

---

33 The national debt is now $281,000 per family, because of inadequate tax revenue to pay for spending and transfers as shown in Figure 5 · US National Income and Federal Budget WW214

SQUARING THE CIRCLE: FULL EMPLOYMENT, STAGNANT WAGES

The simple relationship between supply and demand makes one wonder how we can have low unemployment but stagnant inflation-adjusted wages for most workers. If unemployment is low and businesses have a hard time finding workers, shouldn't they bid up wages? Something like that happened after COVID: employers, especially in low-paying service businesses, had trouble getting workers to return to work, and wages increased for those occupations. Wages for food service and hospitality workers rose about 15% between mid-2020 and mid-2022, much faster than the average for all workers. Workers who weren't happy with their pay and working conditions before the pandemic were flush with money from the government stimulus programs and were able to look around for jobs and pay more to their liking. In short, general labor had some bargaining power. As workers returned slowly to the workforce and the post-pandemic surge in demand for travel and dining out cooled, labor demand and supply came into balance again. The stimulus money got spent. Immigration recovered. Businesses adopted yet more labor-saving technology and practices. And the Federal Reserve raised interest rates to combat post-pandemic inflation. Raising interest rates slows growth and increases unemployment. The Fed's target for inflation is 2%, a somewhat arbitrary target developed during the stagflation of the 1970s. Since that time the Fed has tried to steer a course that keeps both inflation and unemployment low, but if the two are in conflict, the inflation target seems to get preference. Unfortunately, that target results in higher unemployment for general labor. The overall unemployment rate was at a fifty-year low in 2023 at approximately 3.6%. Here's how it broke down, roughly, by educational attainment:

- No high school diploma: 5.4%

- High school diploma only (no college): 4.0%

- Bachelor's degree or higher: 2.1%

We must also remember that the official unemployment rate is based on people saying they are looking for work. People who have dropped out of the workforce, or were never in it in the first place, are not counted as unemployed. In contrast, the "labor force participation rate" tells us what fraction of people are working.

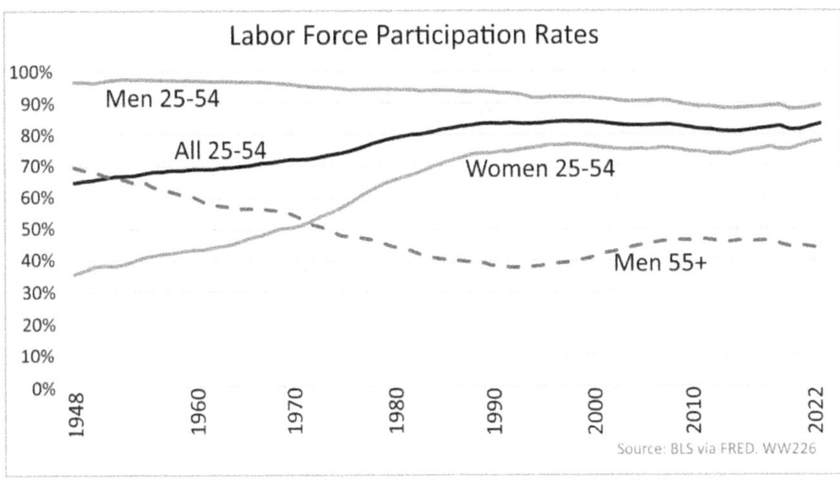

Figure 15. Labor Force Participation Rate

Figure 15 shows the dramatic rise in employment among women since 1950 and a significant decline in labor force participation by men, especially older men. The increase in women in the workforce is yet one more source of labor, far outpacing the increase in immigrant labor. Studies suggest that the entry of women into an occupation lowered wages, but occupational segregation blunted this effect: Especially at first, there were "men's jobs" and "women's jobs." The decline in manufacturing disproportionally affected men, some of whom left the work force permanently. Of prime-age men not in the workforce, some have already retired, some are pursuing education, and some are stay-at-home dads. Almost half of men not in the workforce, though, are officially disabled and collecting social security disability payments.[34] Statistical studies have shown a strong correlation between

....

34 Terry Jones, 2020 "Labor Force Participation Rate Mystery: Why Have So Many Americans Stopped Working?" Investor's Business Daily, February 14, 2020 https://www.investors.com/news/labor-force-participation-rate-low/.

factory closures and increased disability claims.[35] People on disability are not counted as unemployed, and in many economically depressed areas a lot of people have dropped off the work rolls, whether "disabled" or not.

In other words, the official unemployment rate doesn't accurately reflect the surplus of labor, since part of that surplus simply disappears from the labor market.

The original question was why low unemployment doesn't drive up wages. The answer is that the unemployment rate for general labor is higher than overall unemployment, that even that unemployment rate is an undercount because some prime-working-age men have left the workforce, that demand for general labor is constantly under attack from automation, that the supply of labor has increased as women have entered the workforce, that a steady inflow of migrants continuously refreshes the pool of general labor, that trade, while it lowers prices and effectively increases wages, lowers labor's bargaining power, and that union membership has declined and gig work increased. A better question might be why haven't wages *fallen* for many workers?

THE FUTURE OF INCOME INEQUALITY

High inequality of income and wealth are the historical norm worldwide. Modern industrialization and automation in agriculture and manufacturing essentially ended scarcity in advanced economies. That abundance, along with the Great Compression after World War II, brought us the ascendant middle class, which made up 60% of America's population by 1960. But for the last 50 years, when measured around median income, the middle class has been shrinking and is barely a majority now. The lower- and upper-income groups have both grown, resulting in greater inequality.

....

35 The Americans with Disabilities Act, passed in 1990, greatly expanded the definition of who's disabled and increased funding, making claiming disability easier. But a study of a sardine canary closing in Norway shows the same excess of disability claims. In the US various papers by Autor document the trend.

What does the future of income distribution look like if we continue the same path?

Labor productivity growth, by definition, means fewer workers are required to produce a given amount of "stuff," where stuff can be a physical good or a service. We've seen that agriculture only requires 1% of US workers and manufacturing about 8%. Since the combined workforce required for agriculture and manufacturing is about 10% of all workers, further productivity gains in these two areas won't have a major impact on overall labor demand. Both have shown relatively stable employment over the last decade. As we have discussed, even shutting down all trade and "bringing back" all manufacturing to the US would not generate a lot of jobs because of automation, and those jobs would not "pay well" nor in many cases be a lot of fun or offer growth potential, and overall, we'd be poorer.

More than 80% of us now work in the catch-all category of "services," which includes all businesses that don't produce physical goods. Productivity growth in services has generally been slower than in the goods-producing sector, but the category is very diverse. In some services, the human element is really important. I suppose a machine could give you a haircut, serve you a meal, or give you a massage, but most people would go with humans if the price differential weren't large. Artificial intelligence has the potential to substitute for labor in many services. Google's Waymo fleet of driverless cars and taxis have driven over 40 million miles with a safety record far better than human drivers; autonomous trucks are next.[36] AI can also perform many "white collar" jobs or make them more productive. It can read medical scans, write programs, generate written content, perform customer service, make trades, and in general do a great many things humans do now. Like machines and automation in manufacturing, AI will both replace and complement human labor. It's like your washing machine. You have to fill it and empty it, but the machine does all the work required to wash the clothes. That's a good thing. But when applied to "work," we've seen that increased productivity can and does cause job dislocations and can increase income

....

36 It is a testament to headline grabbing that most people are familiar with the failures of Tesla's "full self-driving mode" and unfamiliar with Waymo's success except in cities where it currently operates.

inequality despite adding to national income per capita. It seems as if income and wealth inequality will continue to grow, unless we do something to reverse the trend. The rising tide of increased national income will continue to lift the yachts of the richest much faster than the runabouts of the middle class or the leaky dinghies of the bottom half of workers. The sad part is that we keep getting richer as a country and nobody needs to be in a leaky dinghy.[37] Let's look at past attempts to address inequality and poverty in the US.

37 And the really sad part is that many in the leaky dinghies think the people in the yachts are going to pluck them out of the water. Some of course would, gladly, but others not so much.

3

A BRIEF HISTORY OF US POLICIES TO ADDRESS OPPORTUNITY, POVERTY, AND INEQUALITY

In Chapter 1 we saw that income and wealth inequality, high before 1900, dipped as the middle class grew after World War II but has again been rising since Reagan's time. In Chapter 2 we looked at some of the economic reasons for these changes. Economics and politics are inextricably intertwined. In this chapter we'll look more closely at their connection.

THE GILDED AGE

The British colonies that became the US, Canada, Australia, and New Zealand were all mostly populated by immigrants and convicts from England. The New World offered settlers land for subsistence farming and the opportunity to largely self-govern. While most immigrants were poor by today's standards, they were better off and earned more than their European counterparts. Income and wealth inequality were relatively low in the colonial period as land for farming was easily acquired. As the nation grew after the Revolution, the continuous opening of new lands to the west, increasing industrialization, and a growing service sector kept demand for labor high. Real output per capita, productivity, and wages grew, as did income and wealth inequality. After the Civil War industrialization took off in earnest as railroads lowered shipping costs dramatically, making large-scale manufacturing and agriculture possible. Railroads also opened up the West to settlement. Under various homestead acts and railroad land grants, the federal government gave away 270 million acres of land at no or low cost to settlers. Immigration was encouraged to settle these lands and huge waves of European immigrants arrived, overcrowding housing in the cities. The economic history of the US reads as an exciting story of growth and opportunity. The federal government played an essential role in enabling this growth, acquiring territories, pushing the native population onto ever smaller and more marginal reservations, giving away land, raising and lowering tariffs to protect domestic industries or to spur trade, and actively subsidizing the transportation network of canals, roads, and railroads. The government also invested in innovations such as the telegraph, protected intellectual property via the US Patent Office, and after the Civil War increasingly helped stabilize finances and reduce bank failures.

There is another side to this rosy picture of economic growth and opportunity of course. Slavery underpinned the economy of the South and eventually we fought the Civil War to end it. There were periodic painful economic depressions. Life was often hard on small farms where the majority of Americans still lived until nearly 1900. The rise of trusts and monopoly pricing during the Gilded Age (roughly 1870–1900) fed the growth of huge fortunes and money-fueled political corruption, but living and working conditions for unskilled industrial workers were terrible, and unions grew and fought for better wages, shorter hours, and job safety. As output per person grew, a sizeable middle class developed.

Prior to the late 1800s the federal government played only a minor role in dealing with poverty, but it did acquire and distribute land widely, especially after the 1862 Homestead Act allowed any adult citizen to acquire 160 acres of public land in the West. It should be noted that the government could have, as it had at times, sold large tracts of land to private speculators but chose instead to distribute land widely for free.

By the 1870s, economic growth, corruption, and the excesses of the Gilded Age led to increasing state and federal government involvement in economic affairs. Voters began to insist that governments at all levels curb what they saw as abuses. Farmers in the Midwest, South, and later West, were at the mercy of railroads to get their crops to market. The long-distance railroads, which had been massively subsidized by the federal government, were effectively monopolies: in many cases only one railroad served farmers in parts of the country. Not only that, but the railroads also owned many of the grain storage facilities. Farmers felt they were being charged exorbitant rates by the railroads for shipping and handling their crops. The Granger Movement, originally a farmer's social organization, grew and was able to get state legislatures to pass laws setting the maximum rate that railroads could charge for their services. The railroads and grain storage facilities challenged these state laws, but in 1877 the Supreme Court ruled that private enterprises that affect the public interest may be regulated by the state.[38] In their decision the justices declared:

> When one becomes a member of society, he necessarily parts with some rights or privileges which, as an individual not affected by his relations to others, he might retain. "A body politic," as aptly defined in the preamble of the Constitution of Massachusetts, "is a social compact by which the whole people covenants with each citizen, and each citizen with the whole people, that all shall be governed by certain laws for the common good." This does not confer power upon the whole people to control rights which are purely and exclusively private… but it does authorize the establishment of laws requiring each citizen to so conduct himself, and so use his own property, as not unnecessarily to injure another... From this source come the police powers…

In the opinion, laws regulating monopoly pricing do not constitute a "taking" unless they make a business untenable. Eventually laws regulating freight prices were enacted in several states, and in 1887 these were superseded by the federal Interstate Commerce Act, which tasked the Interstate Commerce Commission with ensuring that interstate railroad rates were published and "just and reasonable." The ICC was the first federal regulatory agency, and it was created at the behest of voters, especially farmers, to address what was popularly believed to be monopoly pricing power.

Industrial workers also sought government action. Working conditions during the Gilded Age were awful. The Bureau of Labor Statistics, which was set up in 1884, issued reports on hours and wages in many occupations. In 1913, lumber manufacturing workers had an average work week of 60 hours and earned $340 in 2025 dollars, or about $5.60 per hour today.[39] Even more astounding, blast furnace workers had an average 73-hour week and earned essentially the same weekly wage.[40] Coal miners worked 10-hour days, 6 days a week, and didn't see the sun from one Sunday to the next in winter. These jobs, and many others, were highly dangerous, and only four states had workman's compensation laws by 1913. Railroad work was particularly dangerous; 72,000 workers were killed and 2 million injured

38 *Munn v. Illinois* (1877).
39 https://babel.hathitrust.org/cgi/pt?id=uc1.32106020334287&seq=8.
40 https://babel.hathitrust.org/cgi/pt?id=hvd.hj2ajy&seq=30.

between 1890 and 1917.[41] Forty percent of industrial laborers lived below the poverty line. Meanwhile owners played golf, lived in magnificent mansions, and flaunted their wealth.

Figure 16. Dining Room at a Gilded Age Mansion.

Figure 17. Living Room/Bedroom/Kitchen in a NYC Tenement.

....

41 https://www.google.com/books/edition/The_Incorporation_of_America/
    cXJhBgAAQBAJ?hl=en&gbpv=1&dq=%22about+40+porcent+livod+below+the+line+of+tolerable%22&pg=PA90&printsec=frontcover.

These conditions led to the formation of unions seeking to improve working conditions, limit hours, obtain benefits, and raise pay (or prevent pay cuts as in the 1890s). Between 1881 and 1905 there were 37,000 strikes in the construction trades, manufacturing, mining, and railroads. Many of these industrial strikes were spontaneous "wildcat" strikes—early unions such as the AFL (American Federation of Labor) represented skilled craft workers rather than unskilled industrial workers. Paradoxically, after passage of the Sherman Antitrust Act in 1890, which was designed to curb industrial monopoly power and trusts, courts often ruled that unions were illegal conspiracies in restraint of trade. It took well into the twentieth century for workers to gain federal recognition of the right to organize and bargain collectively (Wagner Act, 1935) and to establish the 40-hour workweek, minimum wage, overtime pay, and restrictions on child labor (Fair Labor Standards Act, 1938).

Both the establishment of the Interstate Commerce Commission to regulate perceived monopoly pricing and the labor legislation are examples of government intervention in the marketplace at the behest of voters. In both cases the aim is to cure market imperfections: in one case the monopoly pricing power of railroads and in the other the vast imbalance in bargaining power between large companies and individual workers. The impetus in both cases was not academic: Farmers pushed for regulated railroad freight rates, and unions fought to represent and pass labor market rules for workers. Neither of these directly redistributed income, but both benefited general labor.

One last example of popularly instigated legislation to address a market issue: the Food and Drug Administration (FDA). To quote one source:

> The first widespread public attention to the unsafe practices of the meatpacking industry came in 1898, when the press reported that Armour & Co. had supplied tons of rotten canned beef to the US Army in Cuba during the Spanish-American War. The meat had been packed in tins along with a visible layer of boric acid, which was thought to act as a preservative and was used to mask the stench of the rotten meat. Troops who consumed the meat fell ill, becoming unfit for combat, and some died. Roosevelt, who served in Cuba as a colonel, testified in 1899 that he would have eaten his old hat as soon as eat what he called "embalmed beef."[42]

42 https://www.britannica.com/topic/Meat-Inspection-Act.

Thomas Dolan, a former superintendent for Armour & Co., stated that the company's common practice was to pack and sell "carrion." And not just to the Army. Investigations showed that milk was "stretched" with contaminated water, lead compounds were used as sweeteners, canning techniques allowed the growth of botulism, and that there was widespread use of spoiled products. The public demanded action, and the Pure Food and Drug Act of 1906 established the FDA with a mandate to make sure that food and drugs were reasonably safe. For anyone who thinks government regulation isn't needed in a free market, a 1900s diet might be persuasive.

THE "DEALS": THE ROOSEVELT PRESIDENTS

The robber barons of the Gilded Age ruthlessly squashed incipient rivals, entered into agreements to divide up markets, and bribed politicians to pass favorable legislation. A highly partisan press delighted in digging up the dirt on both sides of the political spectrum, lending energy to the Progressive Era calls for reform.

In 1890, the Sherman Antitrust Act prohibited market-fixing "combinations in restraint of trade" such as trusts and monopolies. Teddy Roosevelt, who ascended to the presidency in 1901 after the assassination of President McKinley, vigorously pursued breaking up trusts. He felt that government should work for a "Square Deal" for working people and mediate between labor unions and big business. While a lot of what Teddy Roosevelt wanted to get done was blocked by his fellow Republicans in Congress, he articulated, a view of government's role that was widely popular during this period. A few quotes from his famous 1910 speech in Osawatomie, Kansas, illustrate how a lot of people felt at the time.

> I stand for the Square Deal. But when I say that I am for the Square Deal, I mean not merely that I stand for fair play under the present rules of the game, but that I stand for having those rules changed so as to work for a more substantial equality of opportunity and of reward for equally good service. One word of warning, which, I think, is hardly necessary in Kansas. When I say I want a Square Deal for the poor man, I do not mean that I want a Square Deal for the man who remains poor because he has not got the energy to work for himself. . . .

Now, this means that our government, National and State, must be freed from the sinister influence or control of special interests… There can be no effective control of corporations while their political activity remains. To put an end to it will be neither a short nor an easy task, but it can be done…

No man should receive a dollar unless that dollar has been fairly earned. Every dollar received should represent a dollar's worth of service rendered—not gambling in stocks, but service rendered. The really big fortune, the swollen fortune, by the mere fact of its size, acquires qualities which differentiate it in kind as well as in degree from what is possessed by men of relatively small means. Therefore, I believe in a graduated income tax on big fortunes, and in another tax which is far more easily collected and far more effective—a graduated inheritance tax on big fortunes, properly safeguarded against evasion, and increasing rapidly in amount with the size of the estate.

In every wise struggle for human betterment one of the main objects, and often the only object, has been to achieve in large measure equality of opportunity. In the struggle for this great end, nations rise from barbarism to civilization, and through it people press forward from one stage of enlightenment to the next. One of the chief factors in progress is the destruction of special privilege. The essence of any struggle for healthy liberty has always been, and must always be, to take from some one man or class of men the right to enjoy power, or wealth, or position, or immunity, which has not been earned by service to his or their fellows.

As you can see, the issue of extreme income and wealth inequality has been debated for a long time. That the large majority of Americans agreed with Roosevelt's thinking was confirmed by the passage of the Sixteenth Amendment in 1913, which allowed for a graduated income tax. Passing an amendment is no easy task. Of course, the fact that until then most federal revenue had come from tariffs, and that raising tariffs was unpopular, helped. The income tax on individuals and corporations rapidly replaced tariffs and excise taxes as the main source of federal revenue. The estate tax was added in 1916 but has never been a significant revenue source.

Theodore Roosevelt was from the Progressive wing of the Republican party and faced stiff opposition to much of his "Square Deal" agenda in Congress, but as the speech above shows, he used the "bully pulpit" to press for the Progressive agenda. He was not alone, which is why the period from the

1890s to about 1920 is often referred to as the Progressive Era. While there were many rich Progressives such as Roosevelt, a great deal of the energy of the movement came from the growing middle class. Industrial workers in this period often embraced socialism, but Progressives were modernizers who believed in science and technology as keys to future prosperity. They sought to bring about accommodation between the "classes": the individualistic upper class, the sometimes-socialist working class, farmers, and the middle class. Progressives believed in mankind's ability to improve the conditions of life, in a moral obligation to intervene in economic and social affairs, and that government should help to balance the scales. Women were key to the Progressive movement—seeking liberation from Victorian domestic values culminating in women's right to vote in 1920. The Progressive movement also brought us Prohibition in 1920, a clue to its religious underpinnings.

Reforms and social cohesion can make headway during bad times. After World War I, the Roaring Twenties was characterized by Republican political ascendency in Washington, a return to pro-business policies, and a shift away from Progressive reforms, alongside significant government corruption. The second Ku Klux Klan, using paid recruiters, gained millions of members. It was a "fraternal organization" characterized as "anti-Negro, anti-Alien, anti-Red, anti-Catholic, anti-Jew, anti-Darwin, anti-Modern, anti-Liberal, Fundamentalist, vastly Moral, [and] militantly Protestant."[43] In short it was nativist quasi-fascist group that gained significant electoral success. Because of its Protestant, anti-Catholic membership, it supported Prohibition.

The Great Depression starting in 1929 renewed public focus on the role of government in alleviating business cycle crashes and the resultant unemployment and misery. Franklin D. Roosevelt took office in 1933 and within his first 100 days took actions to stabilize the banks, employee people directly or indirectly through public works programs, stabilize agricultural prices and provide support to farmers. All of these expanded the role of

....

43 Writer W. J. Cash, in his 1941 book *The Mind of the South.*

the federal government in the economy, but the need was obvious, and the measures widely popular.

Later New Deal legislation included Social Security (1935), the National Labor Relations Act (1935), which established collective bargaining rights, and the Fair Labor Standards Act (1938), which created the federal minimum wage, overtime rules, and child labor restrictions. Social Security was not the first federal income transfer program—there had been small pensions provided to Civil War widows and elderly veterans—but it was the first large-scale, permanent federal social insurance program in US history. It established ongoing entitlements (retirement, survivor, and later disability benefits, as well as unemployment insurance) funded by payroll taxes. The business community opposed all these measures. The American Bar Association and the US Chamber of Commerce denounced Social Security as an attempt to "Sovietize the country" and a compulsory socialistic tax. Employers predicted that the Social Security Act would increase costs and unemployment and bankrupt businesses. Nevertheless, the Act passed by an overwhelming and bipartisan majority. The grim predictions made by business spectacularly failed to materialize after World War II. Over time, many in the business community came to accept Social Security, as it contributed to economic stability and consumer demand.

Toward the end of World War II, another major income transfer program, the GI Bill, was passed with unanimous bipartisan support. Faced with fifteen million servicemen and -women returning to the workforce, the GI Bill was first conceived as a means to provide financial support while the job market ramped up. But interviews with troops indicated they wanted educational opportunities, and benefits were extended to include low-cost mortgages, low-interest loans to start a business or farm, one year of unemployment compensation, and dedicated payments of tuition and living expenses to attend high school, college, or vocational school. The GI Bill was a huge success, sending eight million veterans to school in the decade after World War II and completely reinventing American higher education. While the GI Bill cost $14.5 billion dollars (about $200 billion today), veterans who took advantage of the educational subsidy earned, on average, $10,000–$15,000 more per year than those who did not, generating up to 10 times the cost of the program in tax revenue.[44] Veterans created a suburban housing boom, taking out 4.3 million home loans with a face value of $33 billion (around $400 billion today). In fact, the whole economy boomed.

It may not be obvious that both Social Security and the GI Bill are income transfers because they are often viewed as "earned." Retirees have contributed to Social Security throughout their working lives, and World War II veterans received low pay and, in many cases, faced grave dangers. But these programs are income transfers because the people receiving the benefits are not the same ones footing the bill. In the case of Social Security, the current generation of workers pays for current retirees' benefits. Also, benefits are scaled so that even though low-wage workers get smaller Social Security checks, they often get back more than they contributed, even with a reasonable rate of return figured in. The GI Bill was paid for through income taxes, which, after the war, fell heavily on the rich. But as we just saw, this investment paid a huge positive return both in growth and in tax receipts.[45] Most of the American people benefited mightily from this growth, and the rich most mightily, despite their complaints.

Toward the end of World War II FDR, in his 1944 State of the Union address, proposed a "Second Bill of Rights," which focused on expanding the economic protections of Social Security. The Second Bill of Rights included:

- The right to a job with an adequate wage.

- The right to a decent home.

- The right to adequate medical care.

- The right to a good education.

....

44 https://www.archives.gov/milestone-documents/servicemens-readjustment-act and The GI Bill (article) | Khan Academy

45 So much for the Laffer curve

Said Franklin Roosevelt:

> We have come to a clear realization of the fact that true individual freedom cannot exist without economic security and independence. "Necessitous men are not free men." People who are hungry and out of a job are the stuff of which dictatorships are made....
>
> In our day these economic truths have become accepted as self-evident. We have accepted, so to speak, a second Bill of Rights under which a new basis of security and prosperity can be established for all regardless of station, race, or creed.

The "clear realization" that Roosevelt speaks of was actually hard fought. Part of the problem is that while a large majority of people across the country's constantly changing political spectrum might in principle agree with the importance of these goals, there are differences of opinion as to how aggressively, and through what means, they should be pursued. The corruption, miserable working conditions, and extreme income and wealth inequality of the Gilded Age followed by the reforms of the Progressive Era and then the Great Depression set the stage for the New Deal. The Square Deal and New Deal recognized that people wanted government to play a role in regulating finance and business and ensuring that workers partook in the benefits of growing productivity. The post-war boom showed that, if anything, these reforms increased the rate of productivity growth and consumer demand from an expanding middle class. In short, government involvement in the economy had been a major success, and people had seen that in their own lives. It was natural to think that government should continue to solve problems.

That said, the next major advance toward FDR's Economic Bill of Rights would not come until the 1960s. In 1945, President Truman proposed national health insurance similar to Social Security, but a conservative congress rejected the idea along with many other "fair deal" proposals. Prosperity had returned, and there was less interest in social programs. The Korean War soaked up money and was unpopular, and in 1952 Eisenhower, a moderate Republican, was elected to the first of two terms. Eisenhower, while not proposing major new social legislation, continued New Deal programs, expanded Social Security, and prioritized a balanced budget over tax cuts. He played a major role in establishing and building the Interstate Highway System. During Eisenhower's presidency, Senator McCarthy's anticommunist witch hunt, abetted by the Senate, came to a head, and black civil rights heated up as an issue. By the end of the 1950s, the New Deal state had been largely stabilized rather than expanded, leaving many of FDR's original economic rights unmet and setting the stage for a renewed push under a new generation of leadership.

THE GREAT SOCIETY: KENNEDY, JOHNSON

In 1960, John F. Kennedy was elected President, narrowly defeating Eisenhower's vice president, Richard Nixon. In his convention acceptance speech Kennedy described the US as being on the edge of a "new frontier" of science and space as well as unconquered problems of poverty and prejudice. Kennedy was relatively young and believed that government could help lead growth and solve problems. He famously said, "Ask not what your country can do for you—ask what you can do for your country," which was his personal moral philosophy of service and civic virtue. In his inaugural address he noted that:

> The world is very different now. For man holds in his mortal hands the power to abolish all forms of human poverty and all forms of human life. And yet the same revolutionary beliefs for which our forebears fought are still at issue around the globe—the belief that the rights of man come not from the generosity of the state but from the hand of God.

Kennedy only served two years and ten months before being assassinated and, as the quote above shows, he was very involved with foreign affairs, including dealing with Cold War issues, nuclear arms control, tariff reductions, and extending US influence abroad. On the domestic front he secured funding for pilot programs to increase business investment in areas of high poverty and unemployment, much of that going to Appalachia, and set the stage for the Civil Rights Act of 1964, which was passed under the presidency of Lyndon Johnson, who succeeded him.

Kennedy, Johnson, and the public were influenced by a couple of widely read books that revealed the persistence of widespread poverty in an increasingly affluent nation. Michael Harrington's 1962 *The Other America* documented the poverty of 40–50 million people in what was by then already an affluent country. Harrington noted that the poor had become largely invisible in the US, hidden on the back roads of the rural landscape or in blighted urban neighborhoods. He tells the story with statistics, but also from direct personal experience, as a reporter wandering around with a notebook and pencil. Already by that time deindustrialization was responsible for many job losses:

> The other Americans are the victims of the very inventions and machines that have provided a higher living standard for the rest of society. They are upside down in the economy, and for them greater productivity often means worse jobs; agricultural advances become hunger.

Rural poverty, then as now, was widespread.

> During the decade of the Fifties 1,500,000 people left the Appalachians. They were the young, the more adventurous, those who sought a new life. As a result of their exile they made colonies of poverty in the city… those who were left behind tended to be the older people, the less imaginative, the defeated. A whole area, in the words of a Maryland State study, became suffused with a "mood of apathy and despair."

Property-owning rural poverty was prevalent in the South, Pacific Northwest, and Rocky Mountains. The outbuildings and houses were dilapidated: In the case of Southern black farmers, 98% of the dwellings were run down, and most lacked plumbing. The productivity gains that made the country affluent had passed these farmers by; they lived much as their forebears had when almost everyone was poor. Worse, the enormous increases in agricultural productivity reduced the prices of farm products, reducing small farm income even further. The poor also included many of the elderly blacks who had migrated from the south to northern cities, as well as the chronic residents of skid row. Harrington's sympathetic personal observations were powerful.

The other book widely thought to have influenced the Kennedy and Johnson administrations is *The Affluent Society*. In the early 1950s John

Kenneth Galbraith, a Harvard professor, obtained a grant from the Carnegie Corporation to study the causes of poverty in large regions of the country. In *The Affluent Society*, published in 1958, poverty was almost an afterthought. Galbraith said that for most Americans the basic needs of food, clothing, and shelter had been met and that increasingly "luxury" goods and services were being produced by what had become a consumer economy. At the same time large pockets of poverty existed, which he attributed mostly to structural factors such as deindustrialization and the modernization of agriculture. Galbraith was an economist and the main thrust of his argument was that mainstream economics had been developed when scarcity was an undeniable fact and seemingly a rule of nature, but that economics needed to recognize that abundance, or affluence, was the new reality in the US and other rich countries. Economic theories based on scarcity had predicted that unskilled workers would stay poor: Any productivity gains would be erased by an expanding population in a world of limited resources. Obviously that no longer applied in the US in the mid-1950s with the growth of the middle class and the rapid rise of productivity. Both Harrington and Galbraith felt that the persistence of poverty in an affluent nation was immoral. Sure, there would always be people who, because of disability or some aspect of their psychological makeup, would end up at the bottom of the economic pile, but most poverty was explained by where people lived and the opportunities available to them. If there was a lot of poverty in Middletown, Ohio, after a steel mill shut down, that was not because all the people of Middletown suffered a personality defect, but because there weren't enough decent-paying jobs. That sort of technological and cost-cutting displacement happens all the time in an evolving economy.

Galbraith had this to say about how to reduce (or eliminate) poverty:

> An affluent society, that is also both compassionate and rational, would, no doubt, secure to all who needed it the minimum income essential for decency and comfort. The corrupting effect on the human spirit of a small amount of unearned revenue has unquestionably been exaggerated as, indeed, have the character-building values of hunger and privation. To secure to each family a minimum standard, as a normal function of the society, would help ensure that the misfortunes of parents, deserved or otherwise, were not visited on their children. It would help ensure that poverty was not self-perpetuating.

However he felt that this would never fly politically, so he recommended that increased public services such as education, healthcare, and investment in housing and transportation be directed to those living in pockets of poverty to "enable them either to contend more effectively with their environment, or to escape it and take up life elsewhere on more or less equal terms with others." He also recommended "slum clearance" in cities and analogous reuse of unproductive rural land, although he doesn't say anything about how that could be accomplished.

Michael Harrington on the other hand recommended 1930s-style public works to employ people directly in depressed areas. He clearly felt that if people had decent paying work, poverty—at least for those able to work—would disappear. Since there would always be dislocations in a capitalist market economy, government could fill in the holes, so to speak, as needed.

The early 1960s was a time of rapid technological and scientific advances along with productivity growth, and it really did seem that we could and should do something to eliminate poverty. President Johnson had worked as a teacher and principal at an impoverished and segregated Mexican-American school in Cotulla, Texas, and the experience profoundly influenced his views on education and civil rights. In May of 1964, at a commencement speech in Michigan, Johnson essentially announced the continuation of New Deal progressivism, which he called the Great Society. Said the president: "The Great Society rests on abundance and liberty for all. It demands an end to poverty and racial injustice, to which we are totally committed in our time. But that is just the beginning."[46] The Great Society was to be an ongoing effort, "a challenge constantly renewed, beckoning us toward a destiny where the meaning of our lives matches the marvelous products of our labor." Johnson continued to say that he planned to assemble working groups to recommend the best ways to address the issues he identified.

The landslide election of 1964 gave Johnson the congressional support he needed: The list of Great Society programs and legislation passed is only comparable to the New Deal. The "war on poverty" increased federal

------

46 https://www.presidency.ucsb.edu/documents/remarks-the-university-michigan.

involvement in education, employment, and healthcare. The Economic Opportunity Act of 1964 created the Job Corps and Volunteers in Service to America (VISTA) under the new Office of Economic Opportunity; the Food Stamp Act of 1964 provided low-income people assistance in purchasing food; the Elementary and Secondary Education Act of 1965 authorized federal expenditure on low-income schools; and the Social Security Amendments of 1965 created Medicaid and Medicare and raised Social Security cash payments by 23%. Measures designed to end racial injustice included the Civil Rights Act of 1964, which prohibited racial segregation in schools, public spaces, and workplaces; the Voting Rights Act of 1965, which ensured that minorities could exercise their right to vote; the Immigration and Nationality Act of 1965, which abolished quotas based on national origin and placed a greater emphasis on skills and links to US citizens; and the Civil Rights Act of 1968, which prohibited housing discrimination. Additional projects included the National Endowment for the Arts; consumer protection measures; the Housing and Urban Development Act of 1965, which expanded the federal housing program; the Motor Vehicle Air Pollution Control Act of 1965, which limited motor vehicle emissions; and the National Trails System Act of 1968, which created a system of hiking trails. Over the course of his presidency Johnson and Congress raised Social Security minimum benefits and expanded covered earnings and beneficiaries, making the program much more robust, with total benefits growing by 100%.

As we saw, these programs, and the Earned Income Tax Credit added under Nixon, to be discussed later, are the main reason that the lower half of US households claim 20% of national income instead of the 10% they take home in pay. The chart below shows federal transfer payments in 2023. By far the largest cash transfer is Social Security, followed at a distance by veterans' retirement and disability payments, Social Security disability and supplemental income, and the refundable portions of the Earned Income Tax Credit and Child Tax Credit, to be discussed later. The rest of the programs, such as Medicare and Medicaid are "in-kind" programs that pay for specific services or goods directly, not by providing cash.

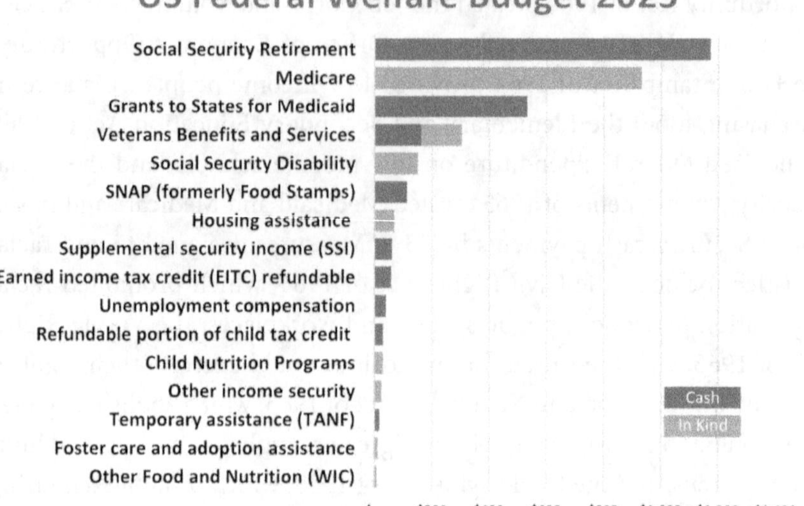

Figure 18. US Income Transfer Programs.

"Welfare" in the context of Figure 18 refers to transfer payments that provide support to individuals and families directly or indirectly. Social Security has by far the largest cost and impact. In 2020 the Congressional Research Service estimated that without Social Security, 28 million more Americans would be in poverty.[47]

Cash payments to the poor in Johnson's day were called Aid to Families with Dependent Children (AFDC), a program established along with Social Security in the 1930s. AFDC, like Temporary Assistance for Needy Families (TANF) which replaced it in 1996, was always a miniscule part of the budget. Johnson did not believe that simply giving the poor more cash was viable politically and followed Galbraith's advice in providing services. Building on a Kennedy initiative he established a "Jobs Corps" designed to train and, to a very limited extent, provide jobs for youth in areas of high unemployment. Project Head Start was founded in the belief that early childhood education

....
47 https://www.congress.gov/crs-product/R45031.

would help boost learning and later employability. Additional funding for education in districts with low-income households was provided. The Office of Economic Opportunity was created to focus on local, community-driven solutions to address poverty with "maximum feasible participation" by residents. Small business loans and support were funneled to low-income areas, particularly Appalachia.

Unlike the transfer programs such as food stamps and increased Social Security payments, the programs to provide economic opportunity and training didn't have much success. Budgets were small at best, and the expansion of the Vietnam War sucked away resources. Perhaps the biggest impact of these programs was as a hidden jobs program. In *The Undeserving Poor*, Michael Katz says that "public and quasi-public employment (service sector jobs and private programs and agencies funded with public money) provided the backbone of the emergent black middle class. They had become the distinctive African American occupational niche, in 2000, for instance employing 43% of African American women."[48]

On the other hand, Medicare and Medicaid had a major impact on the ability of older and poorer Americans to access health care. The huge amounts of money flowing through these programs go of course to doctors, hospitals, and medical staff, not directly to recipients. Despite that fact Johnson faced a lot of opposition to Medicare and Medicaid from the American Medical Association, including a negative lobbying video featuring Ronald Reagan, and sweeteners were added to make the programs more acceptable and profitable to physicians. Medicare is single payer insurance for the elderly, and without it most people wouldn't be able to afford the cost of healthcare in retirement. Until the Affordable Care Act in 2012, America had a system of health care financed by private employer-based insurance for some, social insurance for the elderly, public charity for the indigent, and nothing at all for tens of millions.

By the 1960s many economists had begun to doubt that economic growth alone would end relative or even absolute poverty in the US. Our prior

48 Michael B Katz. 2013. *The Undeserving Poor: America's Enduring Confrontation with Poverty.* Fully Updated and Revised. p.213.

discussion and statistics show that they were correct: growth continued but the distribution of that growth left many behind. A rising tide does not lift all boats equally and in fact some boats sink as technology changes the demand for different types of labor. These economists, concluding that productivity would leave many behind, began advocating for direct income support. Strange as it may seem, the first such calls came from conservative economists such as Milton Friedman, for reasons we'll touch on later. Johnson had embraced the education/healthcare/services approach in his "war on poverty" and was not receptive to direct cash income support, so he did what leaders do when they want to put something off: he created a committee. The Heineman Commission, appointed in January 1968, released its report, *Poverty Amid Plenty: The American Paradox*, in November of 1969. The Commission was hardly a socialist working group, it included the chairman of the board of IBM, the president of Northwest Industries, the president of Equitable Life Assurance Society, the chairman of the Westinghouse Electrical Corporation, and the chairman of the Republic National Bank of Dallas, as well as union officials, economists, and politicians. To quote from *The Undeserving Poor*:

> The commission's main recommendation was *"the development of a universal income supplement program to be administered by the federal government, making payments to all members of the population with income needs."* Most people were poor because they *"lack money and most of them cannot increase their incomes"*; only the government had the resources to provide *"some minimum to all in need."* The Commission stressed that poverty did not result from personal failings and offered a blistering criticism of existing welfare programs which failed to provide adequate support or incentives and demeaned recipients.... The obsolete assumption which considered employment and receipt of welfare *"mutually exclusive had become untenable in a world where many employable persons have potential earnings below assistance payment standards."*

Why would businessmen, some presumably conservative, support a guaranteed basic income? Mostly because of its market orientation. Basically, the Commission felt that low paying work was an inevitable byproduct of automation but recognized that labor is unlike other "factors of production" such as capital and raw materials. People need a reasonable standard of living for many reasons. If people are given cash instead of in-kind services, they buy what they need and want in the market, so less bureaucracy is involved, and efficiency is enhanced. If transfers set a floor under low wages, the market can determine pay levels, perhaps reducing the need for a livable minimum wage.[49] Finally, a properly designed income support would not disincentivize work as some traditional welfare programs were alleged to do. For these reasons, some conservative economists favored a guaranteed basic income. Progressive economists also favored the idea but wanted to see a higher level of basic support.

Republican Richard Nixon won the election of 1968 after a chaotic year of race riots, protests against the war in Vietnam, Johnson withdrawing his candidacy, and Martin Luther King Jr. and Robert F. Kennedy being assassinated. In that election, George Wallace, running a third-party campaign on a racist/populist platform, won the Deep South, while the Democratic slate of Hubert Humphrey and Edmund Muskie won in Texas, much of the Northeast, and a couple of Rust Belt states. Nixon is considered to have been a pragmatic moderate. Rhetorically he appealed to the "silent majority" with an emphasis on law and order and a "war on drugs," and some say coded racism. Otherwise, his actual domestic policy was pretty much a continuation of Johnson's: he created the Environmental Protection Agency and signed the Clean Air Act, proposed a national health insurance plan like the later Obamacare, initiated the first affirmative action program, and expanded and increased Social Security, Medicare, and Food Stamps. He also proposed a guaranteed basic income called the "Family Assistance Plan" (FAP), similar to the recommendation of the Heineman Commission but limited to families with children. That plan would have eliminated 60% of poverty as defined by the government at that time and included provisions to incentivize work, two-parent families (married or not), and of course support children. It passed in the House but stalled in the Senate. The FAP proposal is often billed as a modified negative income tax. A **negative income tax** is a system where people with low earnings receive "refund" payments from the government instead of paying taxes, with the payments

---

49 That would require a livable guaranteed basic income. Work income would then be in addition to a livable base.

shrinking as earnings rise. In effect, it guarantees a minimum income while still rewarding work, because benefits phase out gradually rather than disappearing all at once. The FAP was a "modified" negative income tax in that it would have applied only to families with children and had other restrictions. After Nixon's Watergate resignation in 1975, under Gerald Ford, a smaller modified negative income tax, the Earned Income Tax Credit (EITC), was passed and has since become the federal government's main program to supplement low-working incomes.

As you can see from Figure 18 above, spending on EITC is small. So is the benefit. The IRS provides an EITC calculator online: for a two-parent, one-child family earning $30,000 in wages, the benefit was $4,152 in 2024. If the same family made $24,000 in wages, the EITC was $4,213. EITC is credited with lifting many poor working families above the official poverty line, but barely. For a family of three the official poverty threshold was $25,820 in 2024.

After Ford, Carter's four-year administration was largely concerned with the effects of the OPEC energy crisis and stagflation. Oil prices increased from $13 a barrel to more than $34. Carter deregulated oil and gas and promoted conservation and efficiency, which in the longer run increased domestic production and reduced demand. He proposed welfare reform that would have replaced AFDC, SSI, Food Stamps and other programs with a guaranteed jobs program for those able to work and a livable basic income for those not able to work. The proposal didn't get anywhere in Congress.

THE RESURGENT RICH: REAGAN AND AFTER

In Chapter 1, Figure 3, we saw that the share of national income going to those in the lower 90% of the income scale increased until around the time of Reagan but since then has decreased while income going to the top 10% has risen sharply. In Figure 4 we saw that in inflation-adjusted terms, national income per worker has kept growing uninterrupted but that individual wages have not. Both sets of data are pre-tax and -benefits. In

Chapter 2, "The Reagan Revolution," we saw some of the economic reasons for this change.

Until the "Reagan Revolution" at least lip service was given to the concept of reducing inequality and poverty. There was also widespread agreement among economists that automation would continue to eat into the demand for what I have been calling general labor, and that the only real fix, assuming a fix was desired, was increased income transfers. Even full employment would not guarantee that many workers would not endure functional poverty, so programs like the Earned Income Tax Credit were instituted to supplement low wages. Reagan marked a decisive turning point away from the ideals of the New Deal. What caused this change? US voters were disgusted by stories of "welfare queens" living on the public dole, supporting families with absent fathers. The main cash welfare program of the time was Aid to Families with Dependent Children, established along with Social Security in 1935. AFDC created incentives to have children and disincentives to marriage. The program was largely funded by the federal government but administered by the states, and in many states, AFDC also discouraged work: every dollar earned working reduced AFDC payments by a dollar or more. Like tax avoidance by the rich, poor people (or anyone for that matter) will seek to maximize financial returns. There were also racial overtones: about half of AFDC payments went to poor blacks in the inner cities. That said, clearly there were better ways to design a program to support the poor. The Heineman Commission had recommended basic income support which did not penalize marriage or work, and Carter had proposed a public works program. Neither was adopted, but the Earned Income Tax Credit provided a minimal assist to the working poor. During his presidency, Ronald Reagan implemented significant cuts and restrictions to AFDC to reduce welfare spending and promote work requirements. Finally, a decade later in 1997, Clinton and the majority Republican Congress ended "welfare as we know it" by replacing AFDC with Temporary Assistance for Needy Families (TANF) which is time-limited (lifetime 60 months or less) assistance to families with minor children and includes a work-or-training requirement. This program carries a lot of "personal responsibility" and other baggage: States, by law, can use their federal block grants for any of four purposes: (1) assisting families in need so children can be cared for in their own homes or the homes of relatives; (2) reducing the dependency of parents in need by promoting job preparation, work, and marriage; (3) preventing pregnancies among unmarried persons; and (4) encouraging the formation and maintenance of two-parent families. As a result, in most states, maximum TANF benefits leave "transitioning" families well below the poverty line and much of the federal block grants are not spent meaningfully supporting the poor. In 2023 the total spending on TANF by the federal government and states combined was around $34 billion which was 0.15% (1.5 thousandths) of our net domestic income of around $23 trillion in that year.

Let's rewind back to Reagan's time and make the broader stakes explicit. Giving money to the poor has always been contentious, but for some the attack on welfare was less about fixing its flaws than about using it as a political wedge to advance a much larger agenda. Welfare was only the tip of the iceberg; the real goal was to undo the New Deal and unfetter business from any government restraint. Since before the time of Reagan a loose group of ultra "conservative" businesspeople and their heirs have used their vast wealth to wage a largely successful public influence and political campaign culminating in Donald Trump. To quote Warren Buffett: "There's class warfare, all right. But it's my class, the rich class, that's making war, and we're winning." Warren of course is a multi-billionaire who is not himself making class warfare, but he knows which end is up. To understand what was, and is, going on we must catch up with the campaign by the ultrarich ultraright and corporate America to reshape the political landscape and enrich themselves further.

In 1965 Ralph Nader's exposé on GM, *Unsafe at Any Speed*, put a focus on the auto industry setting profit ahead of safety, which lent strength to the consumer movement for product safety. That led in turn to the establishment of the US Consumer Product Safety Commission during the Nixon administration in 1972. Earlier in his administration Congress passed and Nixon signed legislation creating the Environmental Protection Agency and the Occupational Safety and Health Administration, both in 1970.

In 1971 Eugene B. Sydnor Jr., education director of the US Chamber of Commerce, asked his friend and Virginia neighbor Lewis F. Powell Jr. to write a confidential memo outlining how big business could respond effectively to these perceived threats to corporate autonomy and profitability. Powell, who would be nominated to the US Supreme Court by Nixon later in the year, was an ideal choice to write such a memo. Clearly brilliant, he viewed environmental and safety regulation as undermining the power of private business and a step toward socialism. His experiences as a corporate lawyer and a director on the board of Phillip Morris from 1964 until his appointment to the Supreme Court made him a champion of the tobacco industry. In that capacity he railed against the growing scientific evidence linking smoking to cancer deaths, insisting that the health benefits of cigarettes were being ignored. He argued, unsuccessfully, that tobacco companies' First Amendment rights were being infringed when news organizations were not giving credence to the cancer denials of the industry. So clearly, he was a man whose "core beliefs" aligned closely with his job and his class's economic interests, a pattern observed often in life.

At his neighbor's request, Powell quickly produced a confidential paper, now known as "the Powell Memorandum." It asserted without any supporting evidence that legislation to protect the environment, consumers, and workers were an "attack on the free enterprise system." This was probably not a stretch for a fellow who graduated from Harvard Law and could convince himself that cigarettes had net positive health benefits, but for many of us it is hard to connect the requirement that cars don't impale their drivers on the steering column in a minor crash with a broad attack on market capitalism. I invite you to read his memorandum, which you can find linked in the footnote.[50] If one leaves aside the over-the-top rhetoric, the memo is, as has been often noted, a blueprint for corporate America, and especially those with huge privately held business empires and inherited fortunes, to steer public opinion and politics to their advantage. Powell wrote it as an

50 https://www.reuters.com/investigates/special-report/assets/usa-courts-secrecy-lobbyist/powell-memo.pdf.

internal strategy memo, not a public manifesto. It was meant for Chamber executives and major corporations, not the public. It only became famous later, after Powell's appointment to the Supreme Court, when it was leaked and reprinted, and historians connected it to the corporate mobilization that followed. Here are Powell's major recommendations. They should seem familiar now in 2026.

Influence in Academia

- Powell warned that universities were hotbeds of "anti-business" sentiment.

- He urged corporations to support **pro–free enterprise scholars**, fund university programs, and monitor textbooks and curricula.

- He suggested building long-term relationships with professors and administrators to ensure that business perspectives were represented in classrooms.

Media and Public Opinion

- Powell viewed television, newspapers, and magazines as hostile to corporations.

- He recommended that business leaders fund **media outlets, publications, and public relations campaigns** to present the case for free enterprise.

- He stressed the need for **constant repetition of pro-business arguments** to shift public attitudes.

Legal and Judicial Strategy

- Powell highlighted the importance of **courts and regulation** in shaping the environment for business.

- He advocated expanded use of corporate legal resources, test cases, and amicus briefs to challenge government regulation.

- He suggested a network of corporate lawyers dedicated to defending business interests in constitutional terms (property rights, free speech, limits on regulation).

Political Mobilization

- Powell urged corporations to engage more actively in politics—not only through lobbying, but by **influencing the entire policymaking process**.

- He suggested greater campaign contributions and the formation of strong **business coalitions** to coordinate corporate influence.

- His memo helped inspire the later growth of political action committees (PACs) and large-scale business lobbying organizations.

Creation of Think Tanks and Advocacy Institutions

- Powell emphasized the need for **intellectual infrastructure**—research centers, policy institutes, and advocacy groups—to generate ideas and train future leaders.

- This recommendation contributed to the rise of conservative and pro-business think tanks.

In 1972, less than a year after the Powell Memorandum was drafted, The Business Roundtable formed. An invitational group of the CEOs of many of the US's largest companies, the Roundtable adopts positions so that companies can coordinate their lobbying efforts. The Roundtable has successfully lobbied against pro-labor legislation, for tax cuts, against various corporate governance regulations, and for trade agreements such as NAFTA. The Business Roundtable supplemented the more aggressive US Chamber of Commerce, formed in 1912, which is known for heavy lobbying, advertising campaigns, political contributions, litigation, and more recent involvement in culture war issues. The Chamber, funded almost entirely by large corporations, quadrupled its budget between 1974 and 1980. You will remember that the US Chamber of Commerce was a vocal opponent of the Social Security Act both before and after its passage in 1935. After the Powell Memorandum the number of corporate lobbyists exploded. According to OpenSecrets, by 2024 there were over 12,000 registered federal lobbyists in DC of which organized labor employed 157. Lobbying is also done at the state level. The table below shows lobbying spending by business, labor, and other groups between 1998 and 2025.

Group	Billions	% of total
Business	$70.8	86%
Labor	$1.2	1%
Other	$6.5	8%
Single Issue	$3.8	5%

Table 1. Lobbying by group[51]

In addition to greatly expanded lobbying, big business invested heavily in "political action committees" or PACs. In 1971, after Watergate, Congress passed laws restricting unlimited campaign donations for the obvious reason that any interested party with deep pockets could buy enormous influence through heavy contributions to campaigns. In 1976 the Supreme Court, now including Justice Powell, ruled that limits on *independent* expenditures were unconstitutional infringement on free speech, meaning that PACs could spend unlimited amounts of money in support of or against a candidate so long as they didn't "coordinate" with the official campaign. However, contributions to these "traditional" PACs were still limited to $5,000 per donor.[52] Later, in the 2010 Citizen's United case, the Supreme Court decided that restrictions on how much donors could contribute were unconstitutional and further ruled that the right to unlimited "free speech" applies not just to rich people and their organizations but also to corporations, extending a long history of the court assigning the rights of personhood to corporations. In short, you could amplify your political speech without limit using money. From a politician's viewpoint direct contributions and "independent" expenditures supporting their election are a distinction without a difference. So-called super PACs take in these unlimited contributions, often from

....

51 Source: OpenSecrets from government filings https://www.opensecrets.org/federal-lobbying/ranked-sectors?cycle=a not inflation adjusted.

52 Traditional PACs can also contribute directly to campaigns, but only up to $5,000.

"nonprofit" foundations and organizations that hide their donors. They can then spend unlimited amounts on ads, mailers, canvassing, and other election activities, much of it negative. Super PACs can be extremely nimble and pour huge amounts of money into, say, a state supreme court justice race where a business interest is due to come before the court. From 2000 to 2020, traditional PACs spent over $4.6 billion, 71% of that coming from business PACs and 12% from labor PACs. Between 2010 and 2020 super PACs spent over $5 billion to influence elections.

All the above is just one of the Powell Memorandum's recommendations: political mobilization. Money is important in politics, so important that Mark Hanna, who served as President William McKinley's chief fundraiser famously said, "There are two things that are important in politics. The first is money and I can't remember what the second one is." But Powell also called for a massive effort to influence public opinion, and that led to a sustained ongoing campaign that has been incredibly successful. Superrich libertarian and ultraright-wing individuals organized and funded the effort, often through so-called charitable foundations. The Heritage Foundation, established in 1973, was funded by Joseph Coors, once described by his brother William as "a little bit right of Attila the Hun." The Cato Institute was founded in 1977 by Charles Koch, one of the four heirs to the oil-based Koch business empire and a libertarian with almost no use for government aside from the protection of private property, or at least his. Both these foundations are set up as "independent, nonpartisan 501(c)(3) research institutions," which means that contributions to them are tax-deductible and unlimited and that donors do not have to be disclosed. While a 501(c)(3) organization can't contribute to political campaigns, they can, and do, advocate for positions benefiting their donors. For example, Charles Koch, who tightly controlled the Cato Institute, could have the institute churn out papers objecting to regulations affecting his businesses and get a tax deduction for doing so. While specific regulations or legislation must be avoided, it is perfectly OK for such a foundation to crank out papers decrying the costs of environmental regulation or government in general, and there is essentially no objective standard to which such papers are held or any requirement that, for example, they balance benefits and costs. To gain a veneer of credibility, such "charitable research non-profits" have an "internal review process" for papers, but this is a far cry from academic peer review. Papers often use simplified models, cherry-pick data, and overstate conclusions to support an ideological perspective favorable to the business interests of their funders. The enormous wealth of the donors means that such "research foundations" can hire large staffs and crank out huge numbers of papers and reports which, especially in the internet age, compete successfully for attention with other information sources.

Rich donors also funded university academics favorable to their viewpoints and set up whole programs, such as the Mercatus Center at George Mason University, where they retained staffing control. They also set up many supposedly grassroots organizations, such as Citizens for a Sound Economy. A spinoff of that "astroturf" group, Citizens for the Environment, called acid rain and other environmental problems "myths." When the *Pittsburgh Post-Gazette* investigated the matter, it discovered that the spin-off group had "no citizen membership of its own." Citizens for a Sound Economy received funding from the Kochs and the tobacco, oil, energy, and sugar industries, including Philip Morris, General Electric, and Exxon, among others. That single astroturf group produced more than 100 policy papers each year during its run, delivering them to many congressional offices, sending out thousands of pieces of mail, and getting coverage of its viewpoints in thousands of news articles around the United States. The group's representatives appeared on hundreds of radio and television shows and published hundreds of op-ed articles arguing that "environmental conservation requires a commonsense approach that limits the scope of government," acid rain is a "so-called threat [that] is largely nonexistent," and global warming is "a verdict in search of evidence."[53] A later iteration of this organization was a heavy funder of the Tea Party movement, which was an astroturf creation of Koch Industries and Big Tobacco.[54]

....

53   You can find references for these quotes at https://en.wikipedia.org/wiki/Citizens_for_a_Sound_Economy.
54   https://time.com/secret-origins-of-the-tea-party.

This avalanche of money, cleverly and strategically directed, paid huge dividends for corporations and rich inheritors, in the trillions of dollars annually. By the time of Reagan's election in 1980, trust in government had fallen behind trust in business for the first time.

Since Reagan was the ideal candidate for the resurgent rich in 1980, it is interesting to look a bit at his background. Reagan was a true believer in far-right principles and sometimes conspiracy theories, but, as with astrology and his Christian faith, he was pragmatic in applying his beliefs in politics. Reagan did not start out "conservative." He grew up poor in Dixon, Illinois, which was staunchly Republican at that time, with an active KKK. But Jack Reagan, Ronald's father, remained a populist Democrat who supported unionism and the New Deal. His mother was a devout Christian with an artistic bent. Reagan inherited his acting gene from his mother, who early on involved him in church productions where he discovered that he loved the audience's applause. Reagan's desire for popularity, and his knack for winning it, would inform his later political pragmatism.

Reagan was both ambitious and talented, and his political, social, and economic beliefs evolved over time. While an actor and head of the Screen Actors Guild, he became an anti-communist and FBI informant during the witch hunts of the late 1940s and early 1950s but he was still economically a New Dealer in 1947. To quote a recent biography:

> Reagan complained that the Republican Congress elected in 1946 had passed "tax reduction bills ... to benefit the higher income brackets alone"; "snatched away" Social Security benefits "from almost a million workers"; and "in the false name of economy, millions of children have been deprived of milk once provided through the federal school lunch program." "This is why we must have new faces in the Congress of the United States — Democratic faces."[55]

However, by 1960 he had become a laissez-faire hardliner, calling Kennedy a closet Marxist and being a subscriber to the right-wing *National Review* magazine and friend of its editor, William Buckley, Jr. Like most of us, Reagan's evolving beliefs were based on his experiences, contacts, and financial interests. As Reagan's A-list career dwindled, he resented the high

....

55 Max Root, 2024. Reagan, His Life and Legend, p. 250.

marginal tax rate of the time—he was being paid the current equivalent of $2 million annually. In 1954, the head of MCA, the agency representing Reagan, offered him the opportunity to host *General Electric Theater*, a weekly TV show, for the same salary. While all he had to do was say a few words at the beginning and end of the show, the contract also called for him to travel the country visiting GE plants as part of the company's Employee and Community Relations Program. It turned out that Reagan, who travelled by train because of a fear of flying, was a talented public speaker. GE's leadership at the time was quite right-wing and anti-union, and Reagan's talks, which were scripted by him, were shaped to promote private enterprise and free-market ideals. On the long train rides he read books recommended or assigned by GE's public-relations department, such as John T. Flynn's *The Road Ahead: America's Creeping Revolution*, which warned that "we are being drawn into socialism on the British gradualist model," Friedrich Hayek's *The Road to Serfdom* (1944), and Whittaker Chambers's *Witness* (1952). Over time Reagan's speeches to GE workers and other groups came to include anti-union sentiment, criticism of the New Deal and "big government," including Social Security, and opposition to the socialized medicine programs of Medicare and Medicaid. There was also a healthy dose of racism in the *National Review* articles he read—William F. Buckley wrote editorials weighing in against civil rights legislation and desegregation.

Reagan's appearances on television gave him national stature, and his many public speaking appearances honed his ability to connect with audiences. His speech at Barry Goldwater's nomination in 1964 made him a conservative idol. Ronald and his wife, Nancy, had been gathering a group of political friends who became his "kitchen cabinet" and largely financed his run for the California governorship in 1966. These included drugstore magnate Justin Dart, Ford dealer Holmes Tuttle, land developer William Wilson, and beer mogul Joseph Coors. You may recall that Joseph Coors ("to the right of Attila the Hun") was the founder of the American Heritage Institute. Reagan's campaign speeches, while they mentioned lower taxes and spending, focused heavily on issues of crime and campus unrest, which his travels had taught him were uppermost in the minds of voters.

As governor of California, Reagan's pragmatic side showed itself. During his first months he signed on to the largest budget and tax hike in California history. Later he agreed to tax withholding, something he said he never would do. On social issues, he passed a bill expanding abortion access and signed an act barring open carry of loaded guns (although that was to prevent the Black Panthers from doing so). All in all, Reagan governed California as a moderate and was quite popular, and not just with conservatives.

When Reagan was elected president in 1980, he brought his "kitchen cabinet" and some of his pragmatism with him. Despite all his anti-communist rhetoric, he met with Gorbachev and negotiated a nuclear arms treaty with the USSR in his second term. His key advisors and chief of staff Jim Baker are considered to have been moderate Republicans. While Reagan heavily cut taxes, especially for the wealthy, he also increased spending, leading to large deficits. When the "ultra-pure conservatives," to quote Reagan, demanded his chief of staff, Baker, be replaced because he'd supported a bill tightening tax loopholes to reduce the deficit, Reagan defended him, saying, "Those bastards will never be satisfied."[56]

Reagan's analysis was undoubtably correct, as history has shown, but he still delivered in a big way for the conservatives of that era, starting with income taxes. During the Reagan presidency the top marginal income tax rate was lowered from 73% when he was elected to 28% at the end of his presidency, a huge reduction for the super wealthy. By 1988 there were only two tax brackets: The top 28% rate was applied to income over $79,000 for couples, $48,000 for singles (in 2024 dollars), hitting the middle class. A 15% rate was applied to income below that level. Couples earning less than $13,000 in 2024 dollars who had paid nothing prior to Reagan's election paid the 15% rate.

To try to balance the budget, these tax cuts were partially offset by cuts to programs for the poor. Up to 500,000 families lost AFDC entirely and 300,000 had their benefits reduced; only 45% of the jobless in 1982 received unemployment benefits compared to 76% before. A 40% cut in funding

....

56 Max Boot, 2024, *Reagan: His Life and Legend*, p 742

for the school lunch program required milk servings to be reduced from 6 ounces to 4, and ketchup and relish were counted as vegetables. The homeless crisis took off too:

> There were growing numbers of homeless people in major cities in part because the 1981 budget eliminated federal funding for community mental-health services and replaced it with block grants to the states at a lower level. That made it nearly impossible to provide help to the vast numbers of patients with chronic mental illnesses who were being "deinstitutionalized" as states closed old-fashioned mental hospitals. By 1988, the National Institutes for Mental Health estimated that between 125,000 and 300,000 mentally ill people were homeless.[57]

The poverty rate rose from about 12% in 1979 to about 15% in 1983, before declining modestly, but not to pre-1980s lows. Child poverty and deep poverty—households below 50% of the poverty line—both increased sharply. The minimum wage stayed stuck at $3.35 during Reagan's presidency, leading to a long history of inflation eating into the minimum wage: The minimum wage today is considerably lower than it was in 1981 when inflation is considered.[58]

Not surprisingly the combined tax cuts and cuts to social programs increased inequality. In the 1980s, the after-tax incomes of the top 1% rose by 87%, while the incomes of the poorest tenth fell by 10%. The tax cuts, in conservative economic theory, were supposed to increase economic activity so much that they would pay for themselves and raise the incomes of all workers. As we saw in Chapter 2, that's not what happened. The economy continued to grow after Reagan, right up to the present, but most of the gain has gone to the top while the bottom half of households have lost ground. Budget deficits have ballooned.

Reagan ticked off many of the ultraright's asks. In January 1981, just as Reagan was being sworn in, the Heritage Foundation released *Mandate for Leadership: Policy Management in a Conservative Administration*. The Foundation has released eight other "mandates," the latest being the core

....

57 Max Boot, 2024, *Reagan: His Life and Legend*, p. 732. Currently (2025) over half of the homeless suffer mental illness with 30-45% experiencing serious mental illness.

58 $3.35 in 1981 is about $12.00 in 2025. The current minimum wage is $7.25 and was last raised 16 years ago in 2009.

of Project 2025. Reagan embraced the thousand-page document and distributed a copy of it to every member of his cabinet at their first meeting, and later to every member of Congress. His administration soon delivered on this wish list. Heritage had laid out 1,270 specific policy proposals. According to Heritage itself, the Reagan administration adopted 61% of them in the first year. That included greatly reducing research into, and subsidies for, renewable energy—a key aim of the fossil fuel industry, which was a major source of Heritage funding.

Figure 19. Reagan Addressing the Heritage Foundation in 1986.

On welfare, Reagan's "bible" was *Losing Ground*, a book that was commissioned and paid for by the ultraright Manhattan Institute (whose current board includes Betsy DeVos, the multibillionaire ultraright heir to the Amway fortune). The Manhattan Institute not only paid the author, Charles Murray, to write the book but distributed free copies to politicians and journalists and hired a public relations company to book the author on TV shows. Influencers of the day, such as columnists and reporters, were actually paid to attend posh "seminars" the way drug companies often marketed to doctors. Commentators have shown that all of Murray's core contentions were wrong, but the fact that his book agreed with and reinforced common misconceptions, combined with the monied publicity, pulled the conversation on welfare reform in the direction intended by the ultraright billionaires.

Since Reagan's time, there have been few attempts to "eliminate poverty" or reduce inequality. A lot of hot air has been expended on increasing the supply of "good-paying jobs" for people on the lower half of the economic ladder, but as we have discussed,—and will discuss more—the realities of automation and the labor market mean that many jobs will not "pay well," including manufacturing jobs. In 1996 Clinton signed the Personal Responsibility and Work Opportunity Act which ended Aid to Families with Dependent Children (AFDC) and replaced it with Temporary Assistance for Needy Families (TANF). In 2003, President George W. Bush and a Republican Congress passed the Medicare Prescription Drug Act. Louisiana Representative W. J. "Billy" Tauzin, who was one of the chief architects of the bill, was responsible for including a provision that prohibited Medicare from negotiating prices with drug companies. A year later Tauzin was appointed chief lobbyist for the Pharmaceutical Research and Manufacturers of America (PhRMA), the trade association and lobby group for the drug industry with a "rumored salary of $2 million a year."[59] The Earned Income and Tax Credit, EITC, was expanded in 1993 under Clinton, but remained small. The last major social program, the Affordable Care Act, was passed under President Obama and a Democratic Congress in 2010. The US Department of Health and Human Services (HHS) estimated that twenty million adults (aged 18–64) gained healthcare coverage via ACA in its first two years. Finally, the economy was propped up by large federal cash infusions following the subprime mortgage-fueled Great Recession, and again—more successfully—during the COVID pandemic. Both efforts helped the poor and middle class weather these crises, though a substantial share of the spending went toward keeping large corporations afloat.

---

59 https://web.archive.org/web/20151108233850/https://www.nytimes.com/2004/12/17/opinion/the-drug-lobby-scores-again.html.

On the flip side, income and corporate taxes have been lowered, union membership and protections have eroded, corporate and big-money "special interests" have been given free rein to meddle in politics, and the deficit and national debt have been allowed to balloon.

The Heritage Foundation's latest mandate, aka Project 2025, is the blueprint for the current Trump administration. In addition to a thousand pages of policy recommendations, the Foundation created a database of thousands of candidates vetted for their conservative views to fill top posts throughout the federal government. Trump, who is famously "transactional" and does not appear to have any deeply held convictions beyond self-enrichment and settling scores, has no doubt concluded that letting the superrich and their minions run the show is in his personal best interest. While during the campaign Trump said he would ban people involved in Project 2025 from his administration, top architects of the plan are running the government.[60] Russell Vought, one of the chief architects of Project 2025, was immediately installed as head of the White House Office of Management and Budget, an immensely powerful position. He authored the Project 2025 section on presidential power, a plan to greatly expand the power of the office. It was implemented almost immediately, eliminating whole agencies authorized by Congress, politicizing formerly merit-based hiring, and firing tens of thousands of federal workers. Vought, a self-described Christian nationalist, has also called for using the military domestically to control US citizens. Brendan Carr, an ally of Elon Musk, who wrote the Project 2025 chapter on the Federal Communications Commission, was appointed Chair of the FCC. He used that position to leverage the regulatory power of the FCC to threaten carriers of shows such as *Jimmy Kimmel Live* that the regime doesn't care for. John Ratcliffe, a visiting fellow at the Heritage Foundation and Project 2025 author, was appointed head of the CIA. Peter Navarro wrote one of the two competing essays on trade for Project 2025, the one calling for tariffs to "balance" trade. The other trade essay extolled the virtues of free trade. Trump went with Navarro and tariffs. In addition to Project 2025 authors, Trump's cabinet and top picks include 15 billionaires. Project 2025's policy

60 https://www.afgc.org/article/new-trump-administration-packed-with-project-2025-architects.

proposals reflect the outlook and interests of the Heritage Foundation's funders. Tax breaks favoring the wealthy, cutting spending on SNAP and Medicaid, and strongly supporting the increased use of fossil fuels while defunding investment in renewables are in the plan, and were implemented in the first 100 days with the blessing of a Republican Congress. The Federal Reserve currently has two major missions: controlling the rate of inflation and trying to limit unemployment. The plan explicitly calls for the Fed to drop unemployment as a consideration and focus only on inflation. It also calls for eventually moving from an income tax to a national sales tax, further cutting the corporate tax rate, and reducing the capital gains tax, which is already well below most earned-income tax rates. The plan calls for returning to the two-tier income tax that Reagan tried, while eliminating unnamed deductions, which could increase taxes significantly for millions of low- and middle-income households.

Overall, the economic effect of the already passed tax reductions and cuts to social programs has been to increase inequality and poverty. The 2025 tax cuts will cost around $5 trillion over 10 years with a disproportionate benefit going to the top. The benefit cuts outweigh the tax cuts for the lower third of households, meaning they become poorer. The deficit grows over $4 trillion over the next ten years. (Young people take note: You'll inherit all that.) From an economic perspective, it really seems like Reaganomics on steroids. But Reagan wasn't a fan of tariffs, which are costing US consumers around $30 billion a month now, and we're just getting started.

4
GOVERNMENT AND "GOOD-PAYING JOBS"

In the last chapter we saw how the government sought to address the abuses and rising income and wealth inequality of the Gilded Age through legislation beginning in the Progressive Era and largely culminating in the New Deal. This legislation was extremely successful, resulting in a huge post–World War II middle class and unparalleled economic growth. In earlier chapters we saw how beginning in the 1970s, this "virtuous circle" of GDP growth leading to wage growth leading to further GDP growth came to an end. GDP growth kept right on going, but wages started to stagnate for most, the share of income going to the bottom half of households fell, the middle class shrank, and most of the economic growth since has gone to the top 10%. Wealth inequality has soared to Gilded Age levels with three men owning as much as the bottom half of all households. *We've shown that the main economic driver of this change was the very productivity increases that gave rise to our spectacular continuing economic growth.* Automation and machinery have driven down the need for labor relentlessly in agriculture (1% of employment) and manufacturing (8% of employment), with over 80% of us now competing for jobs in the "service" sector. It is basic economics that supply and demand determine the "price" of anything, and there is now a huge pool of labor available to fill general labor jobs. Furthermore, as Galbraith pointed out way back in 1958, many of the goods and services we produce now are "luxuries," not necessities, which also cuts into the ability of workers to demand higher pay. We have gotten to the ridiculous point where there is more than enough to go around to give everyone a comfortable, middle-class lifestyle, but about half of us are barely making it. The prospect for the young, even those with college degrees, is daunting. "Affordability" is not so much an issue of prices being too high as it is a problem of pay being too low for many.

By stating the problem this way, there is an obvious solution. That solution is to tax the rich and distribute the money to those less well off. That is the solution that was proposed by the Heineman Commission back in 1968 and supported by conservative economists Hayek and Friedman, as we'll show later. Such a program, which we can for the moment imagine as "Social Security for Everyone," or more formally as a "universal basic income" or "negative income tax," has the major benefit of allowing us to share the gains of productivity widely as a nation regardless of what technology does to employment and wages. It is the principal recommendation of this book, and we'll make the case for it at length later. But there are other ways to address income and wealth inequality and, of course, combinations of solutions. One is to extend and enhance the current patchwork of income support and benefit programs the US has now, from Social Security to the Earned Income Tax Credit, to SNAP, to Medicare and Medicaid and the Affordable Care Act. These too are income transfers that help the lower half of Americans survive, if not thrive. Europe has largely gone the route of a generous social safety net and provision of public services. Universal healthcare, free education (up to higher levels), strong social security (pensions, unemployment), public housing, free or heavily subsidized childcare, and subsidized essential utilities like water, energy, and transport are common in Europe.

Another alternative to income transfers is for the government to try to shape the market by creating "good-paying jobs" or designing programs to shoehorn workers into "jobs of the future" through training and skill development. Training has almost universally failed to produce significant positive results, and we won't consider it further here. Can government efforts coerce the capitalist market into producing enough jobs for general labor to increase the wages of the lower half (or more) of US workers significantly? Anyone who believes in a free market should be skeptical of this proposition, and for good reasons. But before we decide that income transfers are the only way to reduce income and wealth inequality, we must be convinced that interfering in the market won't do the trick. Let's look at the current administration's efforts to increase the supply of "good-paying jobs" using tariffs to promote the return of manufacturing jobs. How likely is that to do much to alter the employment landscape and wages for workers?

TARIFFS AND "BRINGING BACK MANUFACTURING"

Politicians are perennially talking about creating "good-paying jobs." Funny, because politicians don't create jobs, companies and small businesses do. The only exception was during the Great Depression, when FDR's administration directly employed people in programs like the Civilian Conservation Corps to reduce unemployment and pump up the economy. Governments also employ a fair number of people during day-to-day operations, such as in the military. Finally, governments at all levels buy stuff, which indirectly employs private sector workers, for example in constructing and maintaining roads and schools or building fighter jets. But that is not what the politicians are talking about, although they do fight like cats to get government spending to their districts. Politicians who talk about creating "good-paying jobs" are almost always asserting that their policies will shape the "free market" in such a way that "good-paying jobs" will be created by the private sector. Often it is those who profess the greatest faith in the capitalist free market to maximize growth who are touting such market interventionist plans, tariffs being a prime example.

To analyze such policy agendas, we must review how a capitalist market economy works. In any market economy, there is demand for goods and services, and businesses are formed to supply that demand and, in the process, make a profit. Businesses compete intensely to produce products and services at lower prices to sell more and increase their profits; some businesses create new products and services. The "invisible hand of the market" automatically matches ever-changing demand with supply over time. Competition drives businesses to always seek the combination of inputs such as raw materials, machines, and labor that minimizes cost. I've already mentioned that I'm a great fan of the managed capitalist market system, which is employed almost universally in the world today, including in both the US and China. Managed capitalism is an amazing engine of productivity growth and wealth creation. But you may have noticed that "labor" is simply one of the factors of production in the market, and no business will pay more for labor than it has to. Unless a business has monopoly power, competitive forces require it to minimize total costs. If replacing general labor with machines and a few skilled tech-savvy workers saves money, that's what the business will do.

To increase the supply of "good-paying jobs," government can try to interfere with the market in some way. Doctors are paid well, and we need more doctors, so one thing government at all levels could do would be to make it easier for more people to become doctors. There are several ways to do that, and it should be done, but I'm not going to pursue this example because that's not what politicians are talking about. Politicians these days invariably talk about "good-paying factory jobs" to invoke the misty memories of the golden age of growth following World War II. But those days are simply not coming back. Even if we closed our borders completely and manufactured everything ourselves, manufacturing productivity has increased so much that only about 3.3 million additional workers would be needed.[61] Compare that to the roughly 150 million workers total, or the roughly 44 million low-wage workers.[62] Requiring all sourcing and production to happen domestically would increase prices. The cost per family would be on the order of $3,000/year, with the highest impact on low-income households. Most of the new manufacturing jobs would be in low-productivity industries such as clothing, while high-productivity export jobs in both manufacturing and services would be lost. It is a stretch to say that the new jobs would be "good-paying": starting factory pay is around $17 per hour. Less dramatically, as we mentioned in the section on deindustrialization, closing the trade deficit could generate two million manufacturing jobs. Manufacturing jobs can also be "reshored" through incentive programs. Industrial policy consistent with international trade rules makes some sense but will not drastically reshape the labor landscape.

In short, fooling around with trade will not change the demand for "general labor" much and will have little effect on wage distribution. Except that increasing prices will effectively reduce real incomes, overall productivity, and real GDP per person.

....

61 https://thoughtleadership.cibc.com/article/can-or-should-the-us-bring-the-factory-jobs-back/ This is on the high side of estimates.

62 The Brookings report already cited available at https://www.brookings.edu/articles/meet-the-low-wage-workforce.

I want to put one more coffin nail in the idea that a manufacturing renaissance is going to employ tens of millions of low-wage workers in the US or make any real difference in income distribution. Here's a quote from a January 2025 article in *Manufacturing Today* headlined "Persistent Labor Shortages are Endangering US Manufacturing Output."

> The US manufacturing industry is facing a perfect storm of demographic, economic, and societal challenges that have contributed to labor shortages. Among the most pressing issues is the retirement of baby boomers. This generation represents a significant portion of the current manufacturing workforce, with nearly 25% of workers over 55.
>
> Compounding the issue is a shift in career preferences among younger generations. Despite competitive pay and benefits in many manufacturing roles, the sector struggles to attract millennials and Gen Z workers.
>
> Some manufacturers have attempted to mitigate these challenges by adopting automation technologies to reduce their reliance on human labor. While automation can improve efficiency and fill some labor gaps, it is not a silver bullet. Operating and maintaining advanced machinery often requires skilled technicians, which means the labor shortage simply shifts to a different, equally critical part of the workforce.
>
> Finally, regional disparities exacerbate the problem. Manufacturing hubs in the Midwest and Southern US are among the hardest hit by labor shortages, with rural areas facing an uphill battle in attracting skilled workers. These regions often lack the infrastructure, education systems, and resources needed to develop a robust local talent pipeline, making it difficult to keep up with labor demand.[63]

Also in early 2025, The Canadian Imperial Bank of Commerce put out a report titled "Can, or should, the US bring the factory jobs back?" A few quotes from that follow. After pointing out that the US entered 2025 essentially at full employment, they say:

> So, we're not talking about increasing total employment or absorbing an overhang of Americans looking for work. Gains in manufacturing jobs, and particularly, in the kind of manufacturing jobs that have now been supplanted by imported goods, would have to entail reallocating workers

---

63 "Persistent Labor Shortages Are Endangering US Manufacturing Output," 2025, *Manufacturing Today*. January 15, 2025. https://manufacturing-today.com/news/persistent-labor-shortages-are-endangering-us-manufacturing-output/.

from other sectors. The evidence suggests that such a reallocation would not, in fact, represent a clear improvement in American living standards.

… the notion that factory jobs carry higher pay is also a historical anachronism. Average hourly wages in manufacturing stopped topping average private sector pay a decade ago, and that gap has been widening since the pandemic, despite the fact that robots replaced some of the lower paid positions on assembly lines.

There's a tendency to romanticize the glory days of manufacturing employment from decades ago. But it's worth remembering that meat packing plants, or rows of sewing machine operators making t-shirts, are also part of the manufacturing sector, and while they are welcome sources of employment for some, today's younger workers are more likely to see their ideal employer elsewhere.[64]

Not only won't additional manufacturing employ a lot of people, but we're already having trouble finding enough workers for the manufacturing we do have. "Bringing back" low-productivity manufacturing by increasing trade tariffs is a great way to mess up the high-productivity manufacturing and service jobs we currently support and export. Yes, the populist right and many on the left have something in common. They're both wrong in thinking that we can create a lot of "good-paying manufacturing jobs," period, let alone by messing with trade. International trade benefits the US—it only requires modifications to ensure it works well. Governments, including the US, regularly engage in tweaking trade policies and tariffs. In modern times there are international trade agreements and bodies which establish rules and can be called upon to deal with alleged unfair trade practices. The US has had a major hand in formulating these rules and setting up these bodies. Given the benefits of international trade, that is the appropriate approach.[65]

64 "Can, or Should, the US Bring the Factory Jobs Back?" n.d, accessed May 8, 2025. https://thoughtleadership.cibc.com/article/can-or-should-the-us-bring-the-factory-jobs-back.

65 We should address our trade deficit, but as already discussed, that will only modestly boost manufacturing employment. For some ideas on how to reduce the deficit, see Caroline Freund, 2017, "Three Ways to Reduce a Trade Deficit," *PIIE*, November 6, 2017, https://www.piie.com/blogs/trade-and-investment-policy-watch/three-ways-reduce-trade-deficit.

DEPORTING UNDOCUMENTED MIGRANTS

If government attempts to interfere in the market to increase the demand for general labor are unlikely to change things much, how about government efforts to reduce the supply of general labor? Trump was elected, at least in part, on a promise to deport undocumented migrants, and during his campaign said that immigrants were taking the jobs of blacks, Hispanics, and union workers. In Chapter 2 we saw that the belief that immigrants are "taking our jobs" is as old as migration and has surfaced repeatedly in American history. Since America is a nation of immigrants, if that were literally true, we'd be in pretty bad shape today instead of being one of the richest, most technologically advanced countries on earth. One must remember that immigrants are not just workers but also consumers: They increase overall demand, which enriches many natives and creates jobs. It is also difficult to assert that anyone is "taking your job" when unemployment is at a historic low, as it was in late 2024, unless your ideal job is picking crops, skinning chicken, or emptying bed pans.

That said, as we saw in Chapter 2, recent immigrants do compete for general labor jobs, such as those in construction and hospitality, and do affect wages for such jobs. Those most impacted by this wage competition are other recent immigrants and natives who have not completed high school. So, while it is not correct to say that recent immigrants are "taking your job," they do increase the pool of general labor and so affect wages for a subset of occupations. This does not apply to immigrants, documented or not, who have been in the country a long time; they are "like everyone else" economically, generating consumer demand and job creation as well as competing for jobs.

The current flow of legal permanent resident immigrants into the United States is around 2,700 per day or about 1,200,000 per year. This flow, as we saw in Chapter 2, is determined by current immigration laws as passed in 1965 and slightly amended by bipartisan Congresses since. The rules for legal immigration could be changed by Congress at any time, but big business and agriculture are firmly pro-immigration. Undocumented migrants also arrive, mostly by overstaying visas, and are deported when caught.[66] Here are some recent numbers for deportations by year: 155,000 per year in FY 2009–16, 81,000 in FY 2017–20, and 38,000 in FY 2021–24. Internal ICE data indicates that deportations through June 2025 were running at around 170,000 on an annual basis, although "voluntary deportations" add to this number.[67]

Economic studies predict that substantially increasing deportations, voluntary or not, would have at best mixed economic consequences. The Wharton School of the University of Pennsylvania's budget model predicts that average wages would fall about 0.5% if there were one million deportations a year for four years. Low-skill workers, including authorized immigrants, would see small increases in their low wages, but skilled workers, or 63% of the workforce, would see declines. The budget deficit would increase an additional $350 billion.[68] It is important to note that this estimate is for the economy as a whole and does not consider what happens industry by industry. If farmers can't persuade enough authorized workers to pick crops, who knows what will happen?

Overall undocumented immigrants are just part of the total flow of immigrants into the US; they constitute about one quarter of the total foreign-born population. Under the rules Congress has established, anyone applying for a green card under valid family or employer sponsorship is accepted as a legal immigrant. Enforcement of border security makes sense; there should be an orderly process. Beyond that, arguments for and against various levels of legal immigration are entirely appropriate in a democracy; that's why we have a Congress. But deporting undocumented migrants will not magically create "good-paying jobs" for general labor. It *may* slightly increase wages in some low-paying jobs, but at an overall cost to the economy.

....

66 The Center for Migration Studies found that between 2016 and 2017, visa overstays accounted for 62% of newly unauthorized immigrants, while 38% were border crossers.

67 https://www.nbcnews.com/data-graphics/us-immigration-tracker-follow-arrests-detentions-border-crossings-rcna189148.

68 https://budgetmodel.wharton.upenn.edu/issues/2025/7/28/mass-deportation-of-unauthorized-immigrants-fiscal-and-economic-effects.

WHAT *CAN* GOVERNMENT DO TO CREATE GOOD-PAYING JOBS?

If trade and immigration policy changes won't have much of a positive effect on wages and inequality, how can government stimulate the creation of "good-paying jobs" for general labor? The question itself betrays a lack of appreciation of the roles business and government play in the economy. As I said earlier, governments don't create most jobs, the managed capitalist market engine does. But government is essential for that engine to run. At the most basic level, without currency, contract law, and courts, modern business would be impossible. Government also keeps the free market efficient by breaking up monopolies and enforcing fair trade. The federal government and the Federal Reserve have a crucial role to play in smoothing out business cycles. In Chapter 3 we saw what happens to the food supply in the absence of regulation and enforcement. As became clear during the Gilded Age and Depression, government also has an essential role to play in setting a minimum wage, defining work hours, and ensuring reasonably safe working conditions. The free market would "race to the bottom" in all these areas under competitive pressure. Expanding on the many essential functions governments at all levels perform to make a market economy possible and keep it running smoothly is a separate book. But let's look at what government can, and does, do to help the market create more high-productivity ("good-paying") employment. Remember that higher labor productivity brings us higher national income per person. Here are some of the things government, any government, can do to increase labor productivity and national income per person.

One is education. Especially now, high-productivity jobs require education. Manufacturers are already having a hard time finding employees with the requisite technical skills. For example, "legacy" machinists often can't operate computer-controlled milling machines. There is a high correlation between level of education, productivity, and income, not just for individuals but between nations and, in the US, states. Education helps make us more productive and adaptable regardless of occupation. US universal education is credited as an important factor in our success: Our industry is based on scientific advances in many fields, from agriculture to AI, and on the engineering required to apply these technologies at scale. The blooming of the middle class after World War II is partly credited to the GI Bill's subsidizing college for veterans, which increased our supply of educated professionals making enormous strides possible in almost every field.

Research too is important. There is a strong positive correlation between national research expenditures and national income. While companies conduct a lot of research, the government provides basic research on which that builds. A few examples of federal research breakthroughs by year: 1945, Doppler radar and the flu shot; 1946, the MRI; 1958, microchips; 1974, barcodes; 1993, GPS and the internet; 1998, Google (the NSF and CIA funded Brin and Page's work); 2011, Siri. This is a very small sample of the spinoffs from government funded research. Studies indicate that nearly every drug approved in recent years has been associated with NIH funding, either directly or indirectly. One study found that 99.4% of the 356 drugs approved between 2010 and 2019 had NIH funding contributions.

Finally, governments also increase productivity and national income through infrastructure investment and careful industrial policy. The railroads, while privately owned, were largely built with public money. The industrial revolution would have stalled without them. Highways, ports, airports, and the electric grid are all essential for business.

All of the above are government investments at the federal, state and local level that increase productivity, raise overall income, and underpin "good-paying jobs." That raises average incomes, but there is no guarantee that this higher output per capita will be evenly distributed. The more productive automation there is, for example, the more output per worker grows, but the less demand there is for general labor. AI will do for "white-collar" jobs what automation has done to blue-collar ones.

Asking government to create "good-paying jobs" for general labor simply ignores the realities of the market, and it's not government's role. To be efficient, the market needs to dictate what is produced and how. But I'm not proposing that we simply throw up our hands when it comes to the current distribution of income. Every full-time working person in the US deserves to make enough to afford a decent middle-class living, and our net national income can easily support that. But we can't force the free market to pay people wages that don't correspond to the market value of their labor, nor should we try.

5

SHARES IN AMERICA: THE CASE FOR A UNIVERSAL BASIC INCOME

Every period in history is unique, that is the nature of history. The current moment is no exception. But as has often been said, while history doesn't repeat itself, it rhymes. The rise of the robber barons of industrialization in the late nineteenth century rhymes with the rise of the "tech" barons of today. Today's enormous concentration of income and wealth echoes that of the Gilded Age. And of course, the pernicious influence of money in politics never changes.

But one of the benefits of rhyming history is that we can learn from it. Our forebears had to pass a constitutional amendment to allow for a graduated income tax; all we have to do is apply it. It is high time for us to stand up for ourselves and fight back against the class warfare the ultrarich ultraright has been waging against the rest of us since Reagan's time. And winning.

The earlier chapters of this book set the groundwork for understanding this unique moment in economic history and for calling us to action. The US economy produces over $190,000 of net income per year per household as of 2024. We have enough now to easily end poverty, and in fact we could all have solid middle-class lifestyles if income were more evenly distributed. Despite that fact, income and wealth inequality have been increasing even as we get richer as a country. Fifty percent of Americans have little to no wealth, the middle class is shrinking, and nearly half of workers are stuck in low-paying work with little chance for advancement. Our managed capitalist market economy is not the problem: It has continued to power growth here and indeed worldwide. But a market economy determines wages based on the supply and demand of labor, and automation has reduced the need for labor, and with it, wages. We can look forward to more of the same from AI.

Simply put, it is high time to recognize that the market will not provide many workers with a decent standard of living. This was noted by the Heineman Commission way back in 1969 when it called for the tangle of means-tested income support programs such as SNAP and housing vouchers to be replaced with "the development of a universal income supplement program to be administered by the federal government, making payments to all members of the population with income needs." Shares in America is just such a program, except that everyone gets it regardless of how rich or poor you are. Below I describe how it would work.

INTRODUCING SHARES IN AMERICA

What is "Shares in America"? Shares in America is simply a payment that every adult citizen of the United States gets regardless of income. The concept goes by various other names such as "universal basic income" (UBI) or "negative income tax" and has been around for a long time. Andrew Yang suggested a payment of $1,000 per month per adult when he made universal basic income the central proposal of his 2016 Democratic primary campaign. There is nothing magical about $1,000 per month per adult, but I will use that amount for illustrative purposes. I call my universal basic income proposal "Shares in America" to make clear that it is not "welfare" but a dividend on the enormous productivity of the United States. Alaska distributes oil dividends to all Alaskans; ancient Rome distributed bread free to all citizens for 500 years. Same idea. We will discuss the benefits of Shares in America in detail later, but here is a short summary:

Unlike "trickle down" tax cuts for the rich, a direct payment of $1,000 per month per adult really is a "rising tide that lifts all boats." It is "trickle up" economics for a change. We can easily afford a dividend of that size or larger as shown later.

Unlike "means-tested" income support such as rent subsidies, SNAP, or even Medicaid, Shares in America does not disincentivize work. You keep every penny you earn *plus* your Share. Unlike traditional welfare there are no demeaning and time-consuming certifications, and no bureaucracy is required. Shares in America is practically immune to fraud because everyone gets it anyway. It could reduce or even eliminate the need for most other income support programs, depending on it's level.

Unlike in-kind welfare such as SNAP or rent or fuel subsidies, Shares is paid in cash and is market oriented. You decide what to use it for: food, rent, or saving for a new car, home, or retirement.

Shares in America will not negatively impact our managed capitalist market engine—quite the reverse. Social Security, a comparable program, is a spur to the economy. Driving income from the rich to the rest of us will spur economic growth as it did after World War II.

Shares in America promotes more equality of opportunity. There is no doubt that those born to richer parents have greater opportunities in life. Shares helps cushion workers from changes in technology and can be adjusted in size as the economy changes.

Shares in America binds us with a common economic interest: Our Shares grow as the economy grows.

The suggestion of a universal basic income to address the impact of automation on wages has a decades-long history in the United States. Nixon tried to implement it in the form of a negative income tax back in 1969, and economists across the political spectrum have endorsed it. But from a political viewpoint the problem seems to be that many question the "fairness" of everyone getting the same Share regardless of working status. I will take a stab at the "fairness" question below. But another objection seems to be that a universal basic income of the size indicated would be too expensive. That objection is easily dealt with.

CAN WE AFFORD SHARES IN AMERICA, AND HOW?

Income transfers, like, say, Social Security, don't "cost" America as a whole anything; they just transfer income from person A to person B. From person A's point of view, there is a "cost"; from person B's point of view, there is increased income. From a national income point of view there is no change. If person A is very rich and has a lot of income, the "cost" may hardly make a dent in their lifestyle, but for person B, a retiree, say, the income can be life changing. So of course we can afford Shares in America. It actually costs nothing overall since it just transfers some income from the top down. Our current net national income, the amount of value we produce as a nation after accounting for amounts we need to invest, is $188,000 per worker.

Clearly if every full-time worker made that, there would be no poverty, everyone could afford a nice place to live, the US could be a Garden of Eden. But we're not talking even vaguely about flattening the income curve. Let's revisit the chart of household income from Chapter 1.

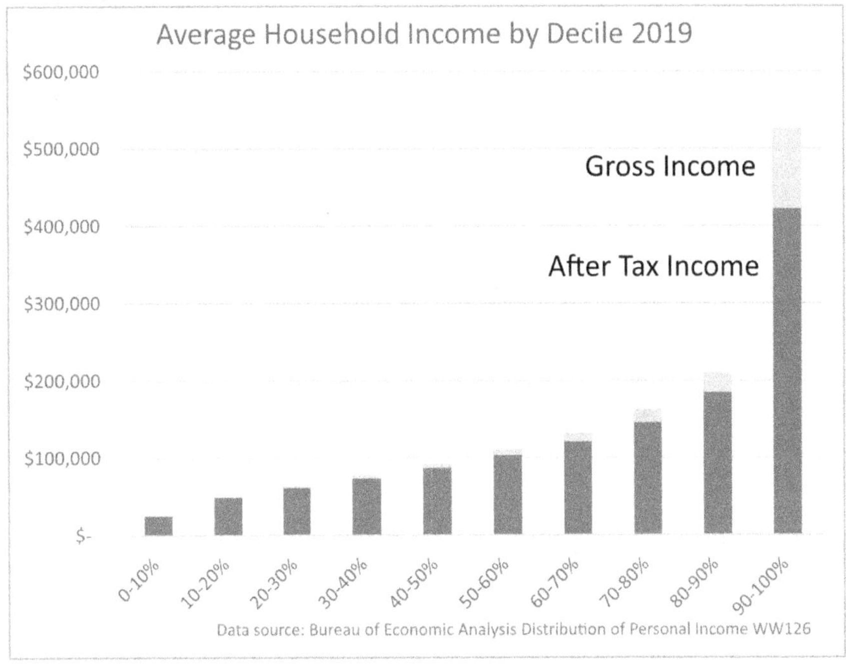

Figure 20. US Household Income by Decile.

Not to be cute, but does anything stand out? As shown in Chapter 1, that top decile is not made up of households all earning $500,000 per year; it is an average dragged upward by some truly huge incomes that would dwarf the chart on their own.

What would this chart look like if we implemented Shares in America for everybody, including that top decile, at, say, $1,000 per month per adult? Below is the same chart with a simple income tax to finance Shares in America.

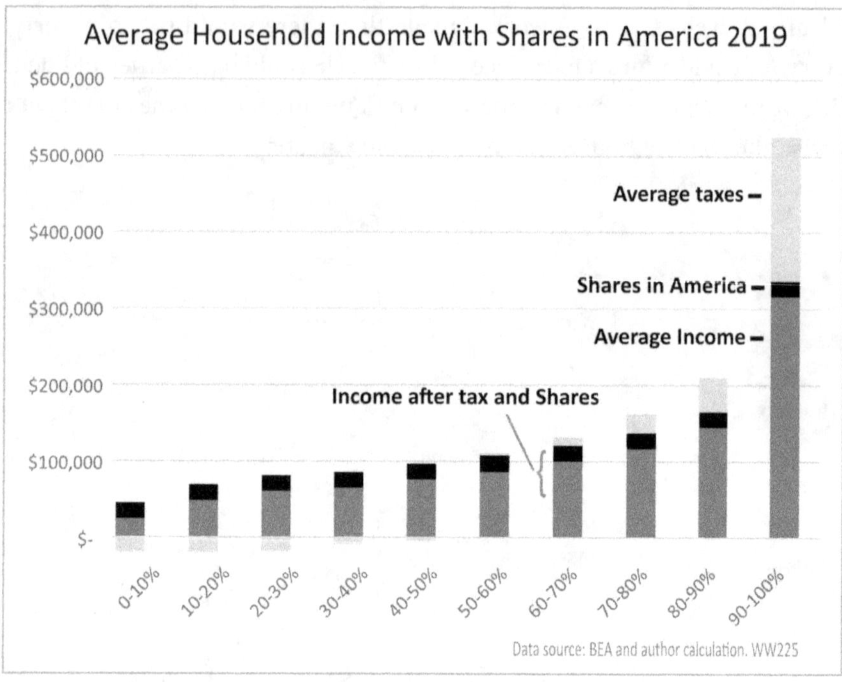

Figure 21. Income Distribution with Shares in America Using a Simple Income Tax.

In this chart, the light shade is net taxation including local, state, and federal, the rectangle is Shares in America payments that everybody gets, and the dark shade is the rest of after-tax income. The table below shows how this graph is calculated using a graduated income tax. The actual tax would be lower for most because within the top 10% there is a huge range of incomes: Some in that decile make $300,000, and some make $500 million. At the upper end, marginal taxes would increase substantially but could be designed so that no family with earned income of less than $300,000 would see their taxes increase. In the chart and the table, the Shares in America per household is $19,200 (2019 dollars) because there are on average 1.6 adults per household. As you can see in the chart above, the small green rectangle makes an enormous difference for people in the entire lower half of household income.

Percentile Group	2019 Mean income	2019 Effective Tax rate	Shares in America Rate	New Tax Rate	Share in America	2019 Avg Disposable Income	New Avg Disposable Income
0-10%	$26,044	1%	0.0%	1%	$19,200	$25,770	$44,970
10-20%	$49,483	1%	0.0%	1%	$19,200	$49,116	$68,316
20-30%	$63,228	2%	0.0%	2%	$19,200	$62,001	$81,201
30-40%	$76,974	4%	10.0%	14%	$19,200	$73,993	$85,496
40-50%	$91,876	5%	12.0%	17%	$19,200	$87,516	$95,691
50-60%	$109,962	6%	14.0%	20%	$19,200	$103,463	$107,268
60-70%	$131,810	8%	15.5%	24%	$19,200	$121,196	$119,965
70-80%	$161,905	10%	17.0%	27%	$19,200	$145,817	$137,493
80-90%	$210,375	12%	18.5%	31%	$19,200	$184,600	$164,880
90-100%	$525,070	20%	20.0%	40%	$19,200	$422,271	$336,457

Table 2. Sample Shares in America post-tax/-transfer income changes.

So, can we afford Shares in America? As we've mentioned, this is an income transfer, so there is no impact on total national income. Yes, we can, without even imposing any real hardship on the top 10% and while making a huge difference to households lower down on the income scale. The illustrative tax used in the graph and table generates substantially more revenue than is needed to fund Shares and assumes no reduction in existing means-tested programs such as the Earned Income Tax Credit. Shares payments themselves would not count as income for either tax purposes or benefit eligibility, so initially they would be layered on top of current benefits. Under these assumptions, the sample tax would fully fund Shares and still produce roughly $4.5 trillion over a decade that could be used to reduce the national debt. This simple exercise demonstrates that the United States has more than enough income to support a program of this scale. In practice, the tax rates applied to upper middle–income households would likely be lower than those shown here.

Is Shares "worth it"? Obviously for anyone in the lower half of the income distribution (and that includes most of us at one time or another in our lives) the answer is yes. How about those of us who will pay higher marginal taxes? My answer is a resounding yes again. You only have to look around now to realize that we all need to share more widely in the country's wealth. In fact it is a democratic imperative.

WHY DO ANYTHING ABOUT INCOME AND WEALTH INEQUALITY?

This is the crux of the issue. Some people are fine with increasing income and wealth inequality. Many are not, including some of the richest people in the country. We've mentioned how AI will be able to replace or complement humans in many white-collar professions, so this is not just of concern to "blue-collar" workers. I asked ChatGPT to summarize the arguments from the web, and edited the reply. Here it is:

> The United States has long prided itself on being a land of opportunity, where effort and ingenuity can elevate anyone, regardless of their starting point. But in recent decades, income and wealth have become increasingly concentrated, raising questions not only about economic outcomes, but also about the kind of society Americans want to live in.
>
> A more equitable distribution of income strengthens the foundations of the economy. When working- and middle-class households have more income, they spend it. This boosts consumption, which drives business investment and job creation. Conversely, when income is overly concentrated at the top, more money is saved or invested in financial markets, which may yield less benefit for the real economy.
>
> Investing in people—through education, health care, and childcare—also pays dividends. A society that enables all its citizens to develop their talents more fully is more productive, more innovative, and more competitive.
>
> High inequality erodes the social fabric. It creates divides—not only in wealth, but in education, health, housing, and life expectancy. The result is a society where the zip code a child is born into can predict their future more reliably than their abilities or efforts. That violates the very idea of meritocracy.
>
> Societies with lower inequality tend to enjoy higher levels of trust and lower levels of crime, anxiety, and resentment. People feel more connected to each other and more confident in their shared future.

Inequality doesn't just threaten economic balance, it threatens democracy. When wealth becomes power, the rules of the game bend toward the already advantaged. Campaign financing, lobbying, and media ownership give the wealthiest citizens an outsized voice, leaving ordinary people feeling unheard and disillusioned. Over time, this weakens civic engagement and fuels political polarization.

At its core, the debate over inequality is about values. Should a nation as rich as the United States tolerate children growing up in poverty while others accumulate fortunes they can't spend in a lifetime? Should economic success depend so heavily on one's parents, neighborhood, or early education?

A good summary, although the speechwriters for Teddy Roosevelt and Franklin Delano Roosevelt we've quoted in Chapter 3 provided a more emotive and human viewpoint.

I also asked ChatGPT for counter arguments. That turned out to be pretty lame:

Critics of aggressive inequality reduction often acknowledge the need to alleviate poverty or expand opportunity, but caution against policies they see as:

- undermining liberty or property rights,

- penalizing productivity and innovation,

- or replacing market forces with inefficient bureaucracy.

They advocate for targeted reforms—like improving education, expanding opportunity, and simplifying tax codes—over large-scale redistribution.

That gives us some benchmarks by which to evaluate possible ways to reduce inequality.

For me, our founding ideals are still my ideals. They include specifically that "all men are created equal." That is simply false when we are faced with vastly disparate levels of opportunity. I understand that given a level playing field some will do better than others, but a homeless kid and a middle-class kid have extremely different playing fields to contend with. One is at a 45-degree angle and full of sharp rocks. Our founders were far from sure our republic would survive as a democracy, but it has, so far (as of this writing), and I believe widespread opportunity has been key. Over time "men created equal" came to include slaves and then women, at least on paper. Vast differences in income and wealth are, in my view, simply not consistent with a broad-based democracy with opportunity for all. That was certainly the argument we heard historically about the reforms of the Progressive Era and New Deal.

Income and wealth inequality are back at Gilded Age levels in the US. Now as then, most Americans feel that we've reached a point in the US where we need to do something about it.[69]

But would Shares in America hurt our capitalist market growth engine? What would the economy look like if we implemented such a plan?

DON'T MESS WITH THE ENGINE

There's nothing wrong with our capitalist market engine. Overall national income growth has been fine, it's just that most of the gains over the last four decades have gone to the top, less to the middle class, and even less to the lower half of Americans. We don't need to do anything about our economic engine, and that includes trade. Don't mess with what isn't broken.

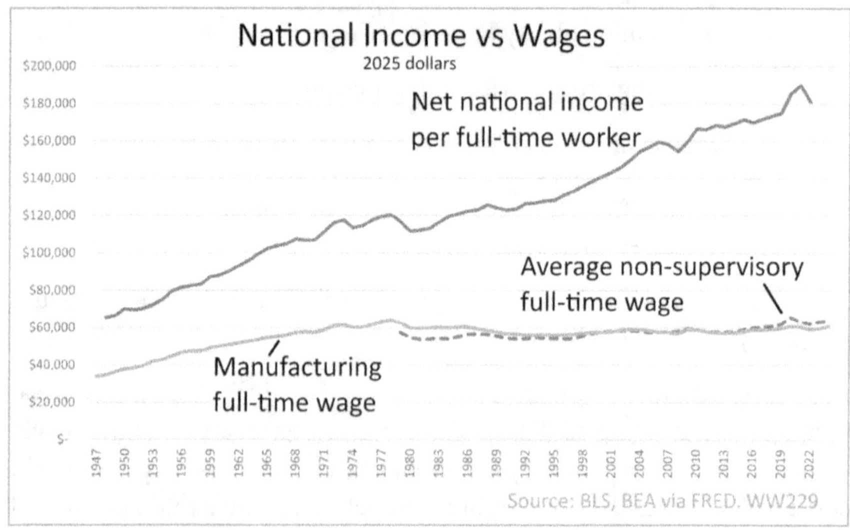

Figure 22. Net National Income per Full-time Worker vs. Full-time Wages in 2025 dollars. Source: BLS, BEA via FRED.

....

69 See these polls and comments: https://www.pewresearch.org/social-trends/2020/01/09/most-americans-say-there-is-too-much-economic-inequality-in-the-u-s-but-fewer-than-half-call-it-a-top-priority/ ; https://fox40.com/business/press-releases/accesswire/922717/the-wealth-gap-crisis-americans-voice-rising-concerns-over-economic-inequality.

Shares in America calls for transferring part of the gains at the upper end of the income scale toward the lower end of the income scale. Will this in some way hurt our capitalist market engine? No, because it won't directly affect that engine any more than Social Security does. Let me explain.

Why Income Transfers Don't Hurt Companies

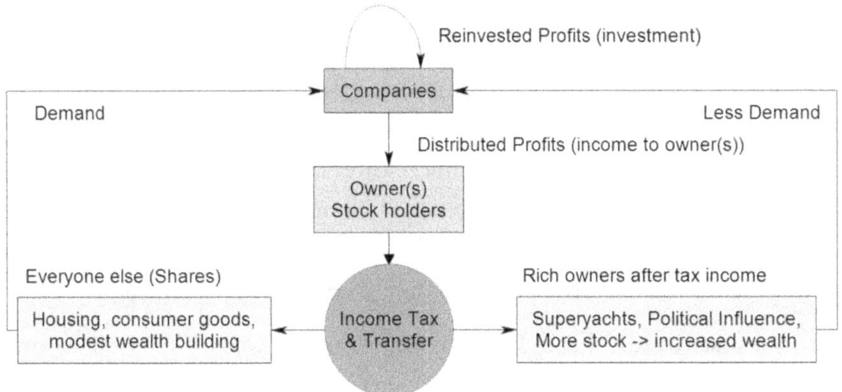

Figure 23. Income Flows in a Market Economy.

In the flowchart above, start with "Companies." Companies make products or sell services, usually reinvest part of their profits, and distribute the rest as income to shareholders. There can be only a few shareholders in a privately held company, or many in a publicly traded company.

In the flowchart we see that shareholders receive the distributed profit as income which is then subject to income taxes. Right now, that income is lightly taxed, so it mostly stays with rich stock owners who use it to buy superyachts, political influence, and more stock, building their wealth. Now suppose marginal taxes were raised and part of that income instead flowed to everyone in the form of Shares in America. "Everyone" will then spend that money to buy food, housing, and other goods, which will stimulate the economy more than superyachts and political influence campaigns. One note: Taxing corporate profits directly at the company level can affect reinvestment, which is why I favor low corporate taxes with caveats.[70] High marginal income tax rates and low corporate tax rates will incentivize companies to invest more. CEO pay, which has ballooned since 1980, will also be taxed at high marginal income tax rates.

Another indication that taxing individual income doesn't hurt business is provided by the history of maximum marginal income tax rates and growth in the economy. Between 1947 and 1963 the highest marginal income tax rate was 91%. Under Reagan it was lowered to 31% and as of 2024 it was 37%. As you can see from Figure 22, none of these changes made any difference to economic growth. A 37% marginal rate might sound like a lot, but that's on the part of income over $750,000 for a married couple. The effective tax rate, especially on rich people, is much lower. We'll get into that a bit later. The point I want to make is simply that income transfers don't affect the capitalist market growth engine; they just move some national income from owners of capital to workers. Is that "fair"? We'll go into that a bit later too.

Income distributed through Shares in America would be used to buy housing, food, consumer goods, and services. It makes no difference to the operation of companies which way the distributed profits flow: they've been distributed. But in fact, shares will flow back to the companies in the form of demand for consumer goods, and that will spur more growth and job creation than if the income is not transferred.

IS SHARES IN AMERICA FAIR?

We've given powerful reasons why too much inequality is bad for society, let alone for individuals. We've seen that we could easily implement a relatively small income transfer to somewhat flatten the income curve without causing meaningful inconvenience even within the top 10%. We've seen that doing so has no impact whatsoever on our capitalist market economic engine. In

70 Some of the caveats include measures to prevent parking money to avoid taxes, strong antitrust enforcement, no accelerated depreciation, reasonable definition of what are legitimate business investments and enactment of much higher marginal tax rates on personal high income. We also must separate economic rents from normal returns; see https://rooseveltinstitute.org/wp-content/uploads/2025/01/RI_Taxing-Excessive-Profits-Competition_Brief_012025.pdf

fact, by transferring this income we would certainly increase consumption, thus driving economic growth. So, what is the downside?

Our politics and a large part of the media at this point are controlled or heavily influenced by monied interests. In the section on the resurgent rich, we saw how, starting in the early 1970s, the ultrarich ultraright organized systematically to reverse as much as possible the gains of the New Deal culminating in the current Heritage Foundation–Project 2025–dominated regime. So, you will doubtless hear howls of how Shares in America is a godless, socialist plot to take away the just spoils of the rich, which will lead, somehow, to further declines of income for working people. Since we've already shown that such an income transfer would no more destroy capitalism than the income transfers of Social Security, Medicare, and Medicaid, the argument really boils down to how "fair" it is to tax the rich at a higher rate than at present. That question was addressed back in 1916 when a constitutional amendment was passed to allow for a graduated income tax: the American people said that yes, it was OK to tax income, and yes, it was OK to tax the rich more. The arguments back then were pretty much the same as we can make now. First, the rich don't need to take "income" to grow their wealth. Any businessman knows that it makes more sense to reinvest profits rather than take them as income. Capital gains aren't taxed at all until they're cashed in, and then you pay a tax rate much less than on earned income. Jeff Bezos famously took an $80,000 salary for many years at Amazon while his wealth was piling up by the billion. He only paid taxes on the salary and any bonuses. If Bezos wanted to have a more lavish lifestyle than afforded by an $80,000 salary, he could borrow money on his fantastic wealth and pay that back at, say 5% interest. The interest is tax-deductible, and he would pay no taxes at all on the borrowed money. This is a well-known strategy called "buy, borrow, die," although in this case it could be called "build, borrow, die." As I will soon make clear, I feel Jeff Bezos amply deserves his fortune; I'm just using this as an example of how the rich can avoid taxes. Second, the rich have many other tax-avoidance techniques available to them, as well as the best legal and tax advisors. Peter Thiel has used Roth IRAs to accumulate billions in tax-free gains. Business owners can have their businesses buy pretty much anything they want, such as private jets, if they can make a case for its business use. The 2025 "Big Beautiful Bill" included a provision allowing businesses to write off the full expense of private jets immediately instead of amortizing them, so there is now no tax on profits used to buy them. Some taxes aren't paid at all by the rich. Social Security is one of the federal government's largest expenses. It is actually a transfer of income from the working to retirees. The amount of Social Security tax on earned income of, say, $10 million paid by a rich person is the same amount as paid by someone earning $176,100, because the Social Security tax is "capped." Additionally, no Social Security tax is paid on capital gains and "pass-through income" from S Corps. In short, the Social Security tax, one of the largest sources of tax money, is paid almost entirely by the middle class and below. In addition to all the legal ways to avoid income taxes, there are also ample opportunities to cheat on taxes and hide money in tax shelter countries. I once read a book on tax avoidance for the well-off that literally said that you could simply decide how much you wanted to pay in taxes, and pointed out that you were highly unlikely to get caught cheating and even then the penalties were low enough that the "expected value" of cheating was highly positive. So, take the official income tax rate on rich people with a shaker of salt.

Given this note of caution about the rich and "income," the graph below shows how the entire sum of local, state, and federal taxes was distributed between income groups. In 1950, the ultrarich paid almost 70% of their income in taxes as befitted the sharing of wartime expenses. They still paid 50% of their income in 1960. By 2018 the 400 richest Americans, billionaires all, paid a lower tax rate than everybody else as shown by the black line with circles.

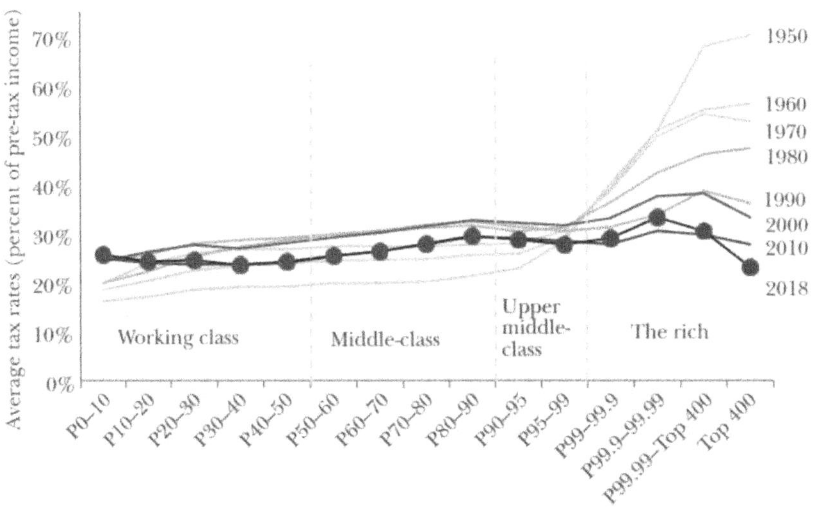

Figure 24. Average Tax Rate by Income Group. Source: Saez, Emmanuel, and Gabriel Zucman. 2020[71]
Source: Saez and Zucman (2019b)
Note: The figure depicts the US average tax rate by income groups from 1950 to 2018. All federal, state, and local taxes are included. Taxes are expressed as a fraction of pre-tax income. P0-10 denotes the bottom percent of the income distribution, P10-20 the next 10 percent, etc.

The graph shows taxes as a percentage of pretax income, which includes all sources including unrealized capital gains. Why do we include capital gains? Because by any reasonable definition, capital gains, which are an increase in your wealth, are income. There is no difference between a stock you own going up $100,000 and you winning a lottery for $100,000, but the first is considered a non-taxable capital gain and the latter taxable income. If and when you do cash in capital gains, you pay a lower tax on that than on earned income. Overall, Americans pay an average of about 24% in local, state, and federal taxes, which seems pretty reasonable for roads, schools, police, fire, military, research, Social Security, Medicare, Medicaid, and all the other programs and services provided. The ultrarich, who have benefited

....

71 Emmanuel Saez, and Gabriel Zucman, 2020, "The Rise of Income and Wealth Inequality in America: Evidence from Distributional Macroeconomic Accounts," *The Journal of Economic Perspectives: A Journal of the American Economic Association* 34 (4): 3–26. Income includes Social Security payments and taxes include Social Security contributions, but most other transfers, such as in-kind Medicare are excluded from income

most from having businesses or ancestors in the US, are now paying the least.

How has the share of taxes paid by the rich fallen so far? Simply because tax rates paid by the wealthy have been reduced drastically over the years. In the 1950s corporate profits were taxed at a 50% rate and marginal taxes on high incomes were around 90%. The tax on corporate profits is now 21% and the maximum marginal income tax rate is 37%. If you're rich you can park your money in a company, grow your wealth tax-free, and pay a low corporate tax rate on any retained profits. No wonder the rich have been getting richer. High taxes on the part of income over certain high levels was deemed fair in the 1950s and 1960s, a time of great economic growth for all Americans including the rich.

Finally, when considering what's fair, let's look at some of the ultrarich ultraright who have been funding such organizations as the Heritage Foundation, which has been working tirelessly to lower taxes for the wealthy—just one of its conservative agendas. As I mentioned earlier, I don't begrudge Jeff Bezos his billions; he built Amazon from the ground up into a business that in many ways has increased productivity and so overall national income and wealth. He largely stays away from politics and has funded real philanthropies to the tune of $10 billion. The same cannot be said for many of the right-wing mega donors. Joseph Coors, who founded the Heritage Foundation in 1973, was an heir to the Coors fortune. The Koch brothers, founders of the Cato Institute and major contributors to the Heritage Foundation, inherited their business, and their political views, from their father. Richard Mellon Scaife, heir through his mother to the Mellon banking, Alcoa aluminum, and Gulf Oil fortune, gave about a billion dollars to conservative think tanks, including the Heritage Foundation, prior to his death in 2014. Betsy DeVos, another major contributor to the Heritage Foundation and other conservative causes, is the daughter of Edgar Prince, who built a billion-dollar auto parts supplier, and the wife of Dick DeVos, heir to the Amway riches. All these heirs to fortunes are also major contributors to "dark money" organizations that can spend unlimited, untraceable, money on influencing politics.

It is a mantra of some of the more generous on the right that they are willing to spend "billions for equality of opportunity, not a penny for equality of outcome," meaning that people should all have as equal an opportunity to rise to their (presumably economic) potential as possible, but that we shouldn't use transfers to ensure that there is a more even distribution of income or wealth. Now obviously there are differences in opportunity between someone who inherits five billion dollars and did nothing more to earn it than being born to the right parents, and someone who is born to homeless parents. Equality of opportunity simply cannot be divorced from economic circumstances. Fairness in the sense of equality of opportunity for each generation calls for more equal distribution of income and wealth.

The primary argument for Shares in America is that we are entering what a young friend sees as "a post-work world," by which he means that machines, automation, and AI keep reducing the need for workers to produce goods and services and that has led to declining returns to labor, and not just unskilled labor. People need and want to work, but a lot of work will not pay well because of the ease with which machines and computers can replace people. Also, much of what humans can uniquely do now falls in the realm of discretionary spending, which limits what customers are willing to pay. This has been going on for a long time and is not going to change. We can all just live with increasing income inequality and extreme and increasing concentration of wealth, and the inevitable loss of democracy and freedom that comes with it, or we can do something about it. Taxing high incomes and large inheritances is not only fair but necessary. I should note that many rich people agree.[72]

There is a flip side to the fairness argument: I've spoken with people who work, or worked, hard and who feel that people who don't work shouldn't get the same payment as those who do. So, while they are fine with taxing the rich more, they are not convinced that everyone should get a Share. The concept of the "undeserving poor" has been around forever, and those charged with administering charity have always struggled to differentiate between the "undeserving" and the "deserving." Life is a crapshoot that starts

....

72   Patriotic millionaires, Warren Buffet, Bill Gates, Sam Altman, Marc Benioff, etc.

at birth—some of us are lucky, and some of us aren't. It is our duty to care for the least of us, which in a rich country means providing a basic living for those who for whatever reason cannot fend for themselves, and certainly for their children. Shares provides such a basic floor, but unlike traditional means-tested welfare is provided to everyone and does not disincentivize work. Social Security supports the elderly with a base income (which, by the way, would be augmented by Shares), and only about 40% of recipients work. Shares is like Social Security for all. I strongly believe in the benefits of "work" for its own sake, and paradoxically, tests of universal basic income show that it tends to boost employment.

WHY SHARES IN AMERICA IS BETTER

As we've seen, by the early 1960s professional economists across the spectrum had concluded that productivity gains would keep down the wages of a large part of the work force. In 1969 the Heineman Commission, composed largely of business leaders, concluded that poor people were poor because they "lack money and most of them cannot increase their incomes" and recommended "the development of a universal income supplement program to be administered by the federal government, making payments to all members of the population with income needs." Milton Friedman, considered a leading conservative economist in his day, argued for minimal government regulation but also for a minimum basic income implemented as a negative income tax. Even the oft quoted, if oft unread, darling of the libertarian right Friedrich Hayek, called for the state to provide "a certain minimum income for everyone ... a sort of floor below which nobody need fall even when he is unable to provide for himself." Friedman, like Hayek, was calling for a means-tested program, not a universal supplement like Shares in America, but in fact the two work similarly, the main difference being that Shares in America is much less of a work disincentive. Friedman's example called for the transfer to phase out in such a way that an extra dollar of income would reduce the supplement by fifty cents, which is essentially a 50% tax on work. With Shares in America, no matter how much you make, you get the entire supplement and there is no net tax increase until you make a solid upper middle-class income, and even then, the offsetting tax goes up slowly. In short, the disincentive to work is essentially nonexistent.[73]

Unlike Friedman's and Hayek's suggestions, Shares in America is designed explicitly to reduce inequality as well as alleviate poverty, but the arguments that those two libertarians put forward for their income proposals apply to Shares in America. Let's look at them.

Maximizes Individual Liberty

There are several ways such a program increases individual liberty.

Unlike some means-tested anti-poverty programs there is no intrusion into people's lives or rules about how the money has to be spent. Everyone gets their Share and decides what to do with it. Friedman put it like this:

> The people whose freedom is really being interfered with are the poor… A government official tells them how much to spend on food, rent, and clothing. They have to get permission from an official to rent a different apartment or secondhand furniture. Mothers receiving aid for dependent children may have their male visitors checked on by government investigators at any hour of the day. They are the people who are deprived of personal liberty, freedom, and dignity.[74]

Friedman and Hayek viewed poverty itself as a form of coercion: Poor people are not free in the same way that people with more money are. But the same argument really applies much more broadly: The more money you have, the more freedom. The choices you make in life—including, for example, whether you opt to be a self-employed gig worker or settle for a job with a boss because of benefits—are clearly influenced by your economic circumstances. With Shares in America, you have more choice, and nobody tells you what to do.

....

73 At higher income levels the tax offset on Shares in America becomes appreciable, but at that level income gains are much higher: fifty percent of a $100,000 pay raise on a two-million-dollar salary still leaves a $50,000 income increase. That seems easier to bear than a 50% tax on a minimum wage job.

74 Milton Friedman, "The Case for a Negative Income Tax: A View from the Right" in *Issues in American Government*, edited by Terry Sanford, 1968, p. 111.

Shares in America does not impinge on the decisions made by business. It does not tell people or businesses how to spend their money and does not increase corporate taxes as envisioned here.[75]

Reduces Bureaucracy

Unlike means-tested programs and other programs designed to alleviate poverty either personally, regionally, or because of changes in employment, virtually no bureaucracy is required for an income transfer program like Shares in America. We have a couple of examples of that already: The Earned Income Tax Credit is the closest we've come to Friedman's negative income tax, and it is automatically calculated as part of a tax return. The other is the very large universal income transfer program we already have: Social Security retirement. With Social Security, there are no strings attached. Live where you like, spend the money as you like, work to supplement it if you want (about 40% do), you get the money automatically, no bureaucracy required. At the time Friedman made his little rant quoted above, the Great Society was in full swing with many overlapping programs and a large bureaucracy. Means-tested programs such as rent subsidies, fuel assistance, SNAP, and others require forms which have to be repeatedly submitted and have requirements that are not only onerous for participants but require bureaucracies. A sufficient income transfer would eliminate the need for most of these programs along with the attendant administrative costs. Fraudulent claims are reduced if you get the money in any case.

Is Market-Oriented

Unlike direct provision of services, when people get money directly, they can decide how to spend it. The market is very good at allocating resources and increasing efficiency by reacting to demand. Take for example housing: The cost to build public housing is often much higher than similar privately developed housing. Another example might be where people choose to live:

75 See the low corporate tax caveats noted in the footnote on p. 81

Right now, there is a large underemployed rural population often kept afloat by various forms of public assistance, most notably disability payments which discourage work and relocating.[76] With a supplement to income, people could choose to stay where they are or move more easily. The cost of living is lower in rural areas and Shares in America, unlike disability, would not penalize working. In fact, we might find that some urban dwellers would move to the country. The point is simply that people could make the choice based on preference, and the market would respond to demand whichever way they decide.

Does Not Discourage Work

This is a key advantage of Shares in America. Everyone gets the same amount regardless of how much they make otherwise. Means-tested income supplement programs strongly discourage work since benefits decline or are eliminated as one earns more. Disability status likewise discourages work. In all cases, tested programs, including the Earned Income Tax Credit, provide barely enough to lift people beyond the official federal poverty line, which is widely recognized as too low.[77] Shares in America provides a net after-tax boost to everyone who is below an upper-middle-class income level, and even for those above that level, the "work penalty" is quite small. Since Shares in America would increase consumption, it will drive job creation, and there will be no financial penalty for taking these jobs, whether one decides to work full- or part-time. Greater leisure time will also be an option, as will taking time to do low-paid or non-paid work, such as taking care of elderly parents.

In addition to income means-testing, a lot of programs look at assets. While it varies by state, Medicaid asset limits are typically $2,000 for an individual and $3,000 for a couple, thus discouraging and in fact penalizing savings.

----

76 There is plenty of evidence that SSI disability is being abused. Disability rates go up when factories close. States encourage welfare recipients to seek disability status since 100% of that is covered by federal SSI while states have to pay part of welfare costs. There is a county in Georgia where a quarter of the population is collecting disability payments.

77 See, for example, https://www.economist.com/special-report/2019/09/26/the-official-way-america-calculates-poverty-is-deeply-flawed.

Shares in America doesn't care about either your income or your assets and so does not discourage saving and wealth building.

Copes with Technology Change

As we've seen, technological change has been the main driver of shifts in employment. Water-powered mills put hand weavers out of work, mechanical reapers replaced human harvesters, and assembly lines with standardized parts displaced skilled fitters and craftsmen. Later, typewriters, adding machines, and telephones reduced the need for clerical help and messengers. Industrial robots took over the work of welders, painters, and assemblers, while computers eliminated countless bookkeepers, filing clerks, and typists. ATMs cut the number of bank tellers, and automated warehouses now rely on robots instead of pickers and sorters. And today, a new wave of AI threatens to disrupt even more occupations.

Each of these innovations made society richer overall, but at the cost of displaced workers and declining demand for labor. Shares in America can help us adapt to any technological change, supporting those affected while allowing everyone to share in the gains from rising productivity.

Delivers Social Benefits

The advantages of Shares in America should be obvious by now. Without affecting our capitalist market growth engine in any way, it transfers income from the top of the income scale down. That in turn reduces income inequality and stimulates economic growth. There will still be a marked inequality in income, but less so. There will still be plenty of rich people, but substantially fewer poor ones. The benefits of the enormous economic growth in the US economy will be somewhat more evenly shared as they were in the post-war period up until Reagan's time. Shares in America builds on a conservative approach to poverty reduction but also appeals to liberal economists. It is market-oriented and doesn't discourage work. In addition to all these benefits it has major social benefits. Here is a synopsis of some of those benefits of a universal basic income (UBI) like *Shares:*

Poverty Reduction and Security

- Direct poverty alleviation: By providing a guaranteed floor of income, UBI reduces extreme poverty and prevents people from falling into destitution.

- Income stability: It acts as a safety net during job loss, illness, or economic downturns, reducing stress and uncertainty.

Improved Health and Well-being

- Physical health: Reduced financial stress is linked to better health outcomes, including lower rates of stress-related illness.

- Mental health: Studies show cash transfers can reduce depression and anxiety, improving overall life satisfaction.

Greater Freedom and Opportunity

- Choice in work and education: With a basic income, people can pursue education, training, or more meaningful jobs without the fear of immediate financial collapse.

- Entrepreneurship: Some evidence suggests it encourages risk-taking, innovation, and small-business creation since individuals have a fallback.

Social Cohesion and Dignity

- Reduced stigma: Unlike means-tested welfare, UBI is universal, which removes the stigma and bureaucracy of proving need.

- Greater equality: By narrowing income gaps at the bottom, it can foster a sense of shared social belonging.

Adaptation to Economic Change

- Automation and job transitions: As economies evolve and some jobs disappear, UBI provides a cushion that allows smoother adjustment to new work opportunities.

- Support for care work: It recognizes and supports unpaid labor such as caregiving, which is often undervalued in markets.

An impressive list. I would like to expand a bit on social cohesion. Money in politics has been a major factor in dividing America. Taxing the rich is popular with most Americans—rural, urban, red, blue—even many of the rich themselves. But it is not popular with an extremely rich subset of the rich, who also find that in the absence of regulation they can make more money by exposing their workers to more hazards, polluting the air and rivers, and suppressing unions. This is in fact old hat, but as we described above, they have used their money very effectively for the past 50 years to divide the American people using whatever means money can buy. And it can buy a lot. They have been amazingly successful at tying their economic issues to "culture war" issues, which they foment. We will look more at money in politics below when we discuss how to get to Shares in America, but for now I'd like to point out that since our Shares in America grow as the economy grows, we will all have an incentive to act like shareholders. We can still argue over cultural issues—that too is old hat—but we have a strong incentive to cooperate and do what is best for the country financially.

UBI VS. GBI VS. NIT: WHICH IS BETTER?

Shares in America is a universal basic income (UBI) program. Above we made the case that guaranteed income is better than, and in large part can replace, traditional means-tested transfers, especially in-kind ones such as SNAP. But universal basic income, guaranteed basic income, and a negative income tax all provide cash. How do these differ and which is better?

UBI provides everyone with the same cash payment - there is no income limit or means testing. A guaranteed basic income (GBI) on the other hand is an income support that only goes to people whose income falls below the basic income level. Either can be implemented as a negative income tax (NIT): in one case everyone gets the same "UBI tax refund," and in the other case people whose income falls below a certain level get a "GBI tax refund," much like the Earned Income Tax Credit now. Both can achieve exactly the same income structure: For high earners, taxes would simply increase to cover the cost of their UBI. The difference between UBI and GBI is far from only semantic, however, even if largely the same transfers could take place. In *Shares in America*, UBI is conceived as a social dividend: each citizen's share of the nation's economic output and productivity growth. Because everyone receives it, UBI avoids stigma, complex eligibility rules, and benefit phase-outs that discourage work.

Times and needs change. Before 1913 we didn't have a graduated income tax, and before 1935 we didn't have Social Security. There is no way at this juncture to prevent increasing income and wealth inequality aside from income transfer. Economists have been touting the concept of a universal basic income for decades. We need to finally come together and get it done.

EXAMPLES AND TESTS OF BASIC INCOME

The United States and other countries with similar retirement programs already have a non-means-tested universal basic income such as Shares in America, only it's age-limited. It's called Social Security. Unlike Shares in America, it's scaled to your earning over your lifetime: the monthly benefit for a low-wage worker after 30 years of work is $1,100, which is below the annual poverty line of $15,650 for a single person, ensuring that if you were poor during your working life, you'll also be poor in retirement. Other countries are more generous with their retirement benefits and have mandatory retirement savings plans. Nonetheless, Social Security has had a huge impact. The elderly poverty rate is around 10%, but without Social Security it would be 37–45%. About 40% of Social Security retirees work part- or full-time.

Aside from retirement programs, there have been few non-means-tested cash income supplement programs in the world; most are designed to guarantee only a minimum income. Shares in America provides a guaranteed basic income but also provides an identical income supplement to all, and net benefits to people well above the poverty line, thus eliminating the age-old problem of who is "deserving" of support and who is not. There is an ancient precedent for a universal basic income. In 58 BC the Roman tribune Publius Clodius established an allotment of free grain for all Roman citizens to help deal with economic dislocations. That system lasted for about 500 years and gave rise to the saying "bread and circuses." In America Thomas Paine suggested a universal basic income to compensate people who lost their right to hunt, fish, or farm on frontier lands as that land was sold to private owners. The US was a land of opportunity, at least for European immigrants, because of its frontier. The state of Alaska distributes a "dividend" on oil production from public lands of between $1,000 and $2,000 annually to all residents. Saudi Arabia dispenses cash from its vast oil wealth to lower-income citizens. And of course, almost all advanced industrial countries provide a "safety net" of social programs including medical care (usually not means-tested) and means-tested income supplements to provide a de facto minimum income. It's hard to conclude much from these examples, but there have been many recent experimental UBI pilots.[78] One of the best designed and researched of these using a control group was in Finland. (You can find more details in the McKinsey & Company article referenced below.)[79] This study compared two groups of initially unemployed people, one receiving just normal benefits the other receiving a modest basic income. The McKinsey article authors summarize the findings:

> The final results from Finland's experiment are now in, and the findings are intriguing: the basic income in Finland led to a small increase in employment, significantly boosted multiple measures of the recipients' well-being, and reinforced positive individual and societal feedback loops.

An article in Bloomberg notes that over the past several years, the idea of direct cash transfers to low-income families has gained a lot of traction in the US as well, with more than 150 local pilots in 35 US states testing the

---

78 These pilots target low income people, so are more accurately called "guaranteed basic income" programs. But the difference between universal basic income and guaranteed minimum income is entirely semantic as explained later.

79 Tera Allas, Jukka Maksimainen, James Manyika, and Navjot Singh, 2020, "An Experiment to Inform Universal Basic Income." McKinsey & Company. September 15, 2020. https://www.mckinsey.com/industries/social-sector/our-insights/an-experiment-to-inform-universal-basic-income.

idea of a basic income.[80] The largest of these studies was funded by Sam Altman, founder of OpenAI. To quote the article:

> After three years of distributing $1,000 monthly to beneficiaries in Illinois and Texas, the organization has released a trio of research papers on its findings. Like many of the other studies released before it, OpenResearch finds that recipients spend more to meet their basic needs and assist others, and don't drop out of the workforce — although they work slightly fewer hours. But the researchers' biggest takeaway is that cash provides flexibility.

They go on to explain that flexibility in meeting needs, for example a car repair, is more useful to people than fixed in-kind benefits such as food stamps in the same dollar amount. In another pilot in Stockton, CA, recipients also mostly spent money on food and essentials, and secured full-time work at higher rates than those in a control group. "Working people know how to spend money in ways that provide for themselves and their families," notes the mayor.[81]

Many of these pilots target very low-income people, but not all. A pilot program in Tacoma, Washington, targeted 110 working people making within 100% to 200% of the federal poverty line. That's a group that generally doesn't qualify for federal assistance but still often has trouble making ends meet. Even though payments were only $500 per month, employment increased in the participating group versus a control group that wasn't receiving these payments, and so did savings and other measures of well-being.[82]

Study after study shows that guaranteed payments improve people's lives without having the undesirable side effects sometimes attributed to traditional income-tested welfare. As a result, support for guaranteed basic income and UBI is growing. Over 100 mayors have joined Mayors for a Guaranteed Income, and public support is mounting as well. Polling in

80 Sarah Holder,, and Shirin Ghaffary, 2024, "Sam Altman-Backed Group Completes Largest US Study on Basic Income." *Bloomberg*. July 22, 2024. https://www.bloomberg.com/news/articles/2024-07-22/ubi-study-backed-by-openai-s-sam-altman-bolsters-support-for-basic-income.

81 https://www.bloomberg.com/news/articles/2022-09-28/for-more-than-20-guaranteed-income-projects-the-data-is-in?sref=Y5NzbMHF

82 https://www.uwpc.org/sites/uwpc/files/24_GRIT_4pg_Data_Summary.pdf. Also see https://www.bloomberg.com/news/articles/2022-09-28/for-more-than-20-guaranteed-income-projects-the-data-is-in

2023 from Economic Security Project and Mayors for a Guaranteed Income shows that a majority of Americans support GBI.

- Strong support from Democrats at 75%.

- A majority of Independents support guaranteed income (53%) with Independents under 50 years of age showing strong support, at 70%.

- Some Republicans show openings for support, with Republicans under 50 years of age showing support at 54%, and non-college Republicans showing support at 48%.[83]

Bloomberg notes that Altman is not alone among tech billionaires in supporting guaranteed income:

> Altman is among several tech leaders like Elon Musk, Jack Dorsey and Marc Benioff who have been proponents of cash payments with no strings attached as a potential antidote to the negative effects of technology automating people's occupations. In 2016, Altman wrote, "I'm fairly confident that at some point in the future, as technology continues to eliminate traditional jobs and massive new wealth gets created, we're going to see some version of this at a national scale."[84]

Beyond the fact that these tech bros are on board, the clearest indication that support is growing for guaranteed income is that the ultrarich ultraright is working to squash the movement. The Foundation for Government Accountability, a conservative think tank, has been pushing for legislation at the state level to stop localities from piloting guaranteed income programs; South Dakota, Idaho, and Iowa all passed such laws.[85] Other challenges are being pursued through the courts. The Supreme Court of Texas paused a Harris County pilot after Attorney General Ken Paxton argued it was unconstitutional. And a similar lawsuit was filed in St. Louis.[86]

Time to get it done.

---

83 https://economicsecurityproject.org/resource/a-window-of-opportunity/

84 https://www.bloomberg.com/news/articles/2024-07-22/ubi-study-backed-by-openai-s-sam-altman-bolsters-support-for-basic-income

85 Major support for Foundation for Government Accountability comes from ultrarich ultraright Richard and Elizabeth Uihlein, American billionaire owners of business supply company Uline, heirs to the Schlitz brewing fortune.

86 https://www.bloomberg.com/news/articles/2024-07-16/child-tax-credit-could-be-a-bipartisan-ubi-compromise

6

RENEWING THE SOCIAL CONTRACT: HOW TO GET THERE FROM HERE

How to get there from here? "There" means an America with more even income and wealth distribution, better able to deal with continued technology changes that eliminate jobs and put downward pressure on wages, and, while we're at it, less partisanship.

In thinking about how to get there from here, I like to divide things into stuff that's broken and needs fixing and stuff that's not broken. As noted often above, the economic engine of the US is not broken, it keeps the economy growing. Right now, that engine produces over $190,000 of net income per household, around $188,000 per year for full time work, and it's only going up from here. We don't need to fix the capitalist market engine. On the other hand, income—and even more so, wealth—inequality is off the charts, literally. We need to fix that. Second, it is widely felt that money in politics is a problem in the US and needs fixing. And finally, most of us would like to see political partisanship toned down. That too needs fixing. It turns out that these three broken things I mentioned are all related: income and wealth inequality, money in politics, and partisanship. They are firmly entangled, and by design.

MONEY IN POLITICS

I'm tired of the US being trashed. The economy keeps on growing, medicine keeps getting better, we have amazing technology, cars and roads are much safer than they used to be, we have plenty of food, lifespans have gone up, air and water are much cleaner than they used to be, we elected a Black president, indicating that prejudice has declined, people are freer than ever before, crime is much lower than it was 30 years ago. And yet there is a major media industry which thrives on trashing the US and stoking "us versus them" divisiveness. This stoking of division is fed by the ultrarich ultraright we've discussed. Here, for example, is what the Heritage Foundation, a right-wing propaganda machine, has to say about crime: "Americans are less safe today than they were a decade ago due to failed models of criminal justice reform, rogue prosecutors, and politicized unequal law enforcement."[87] But here, in contrast, are some graphs showing the actual trajectory of crime rates:

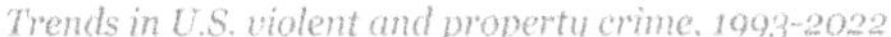

U.S. violent and property crime rates have plunged since 1990s, regardless of data source

Trends in U.S. violent and property crime, 1993-2022

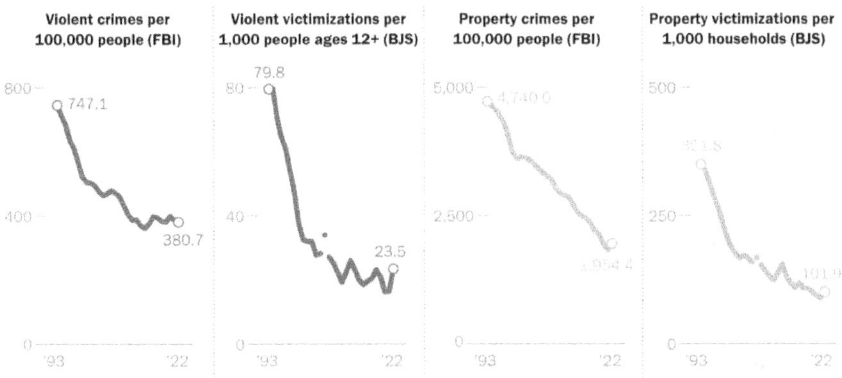

Note: FBI figures include reported crimes only; BJS figures include unreported and reported crimes. 2006 BJS estimates are not comparable to those in other years due to methodological changes.
Source: Federal Bureau of Investigation (FBI), U.S. Bureau of Justice Statistics (BJS).

PEW RESEARCH CENTER

Figure 25. Crime Statistics. Source: PEW Research[88]

One can go through one issue after another where the same kind of misinformation is peddled. Why? Well, in politics as in crime, following the money is always a good place to start. The real aim of the ultrarich ultraright has nothing to do with cultural issues; the aim is to lower taxes for the rich, do away with regulations which restrict their "freedom" to do damage to the country and its workers, and destroy the federal government, which is the main threat to their complete and unfettered accumulation of wealth and power. That requires demonizing what used to be the broad consensus of Americans. In Reagan's day they were more open about their aims. Back then they said, "tax the rich less and the economy will boom and everyone will be

87 https://www.heritage.org/crime-and-justice accessed 10/10/2025.
88 https://www.pewresearch.org/short-reads/2024/04/24/what-the-data-says-about-crime-in-the-us/sr_24-04-23_crime_3.

richer." That of course didn't happen, as we've seen. Instead, the economy kept growing as it had before, but most of the growth now went to the rich. People noticed, and a similar appeal to trickle-down economics wasn't going to work again. So, the ultrarich ultraright got to work, through their highly paid hirelings and foundations, to build "grassroots" movements, as I discussed above. They also invested heavily in political smear campaigns through political action committees (super PACs) which focused on cultural issues. The real aim was always to accumulate political power. The ultrarich ultraright don't really care about crime (which they know has gone down for decades), or immigration (which they are generally for), or international trade (which they are generally for) or abortion (some are pro-life, some are pro-choice, but being rich, they can always get one if needed), and, like the general population, only some want to force their religious convictions on the entire country. But divide and conquer works. With essentially unlimited money, they can stoke resentment and division and sow misinformation using highly paid political operators and dedicated media platforms. They trash America widely. The dystopian world they paint is a fantasy designed to trigger adrenaline and hate. Dividing and stoking hate is the technique of demagogues and dictators since time immemorial.

So, let's all take a deep breath. There is a lot right with America, and we got here despite all the things the ultraright trash. Like science, progressive income taxes, environmental and safety regulations and civil rights legislation. Is everything perfect in America? Of course not, and we can in the due course of politics press our viewpoints at the local, state, and national level. But we can't do that with politics dominated by money. Unfortunately, the Supreme Court has completely removed the limits on money in politics, including by corporations, and it will take either a different Supreme Court or a constitutional amendment(s) to change that. What can we do in the meantime? Vote, of course! We need candidates who are representative of their districts and states on social issues but are also dedicated to reversing the long-term project to enrich the rich. Such candidates can be red or blue, pro-life or pro-choice, etc. in representing their voters, but they should support higher taxes on the rich, a proposition that is widely popular: A

March 2024 Bloomberg News/Morning Consult poll of swing-state voters found 69% favor higher taxes on billionaires and on incomes over $400,000. Support is strong across party lines: a November 2024 analysis of multiple polls found that 51% of Republicans support a billionaire income tax, and a February 2024 Navigator Research poll found 63% of Trump voters support raising taxes on the wealthy. A November 2024 analysis showed 64% of independents support a billionaire income tax.

There is even more consensus on the pernicious influence of money in politics: A 2023 Pew study found that 72% of US adults believe there should be limits on the amount of money individuals and organizations can spend on political campaigns. This view is held by comparable majorities in both the Democratic (76%) and Republican (71%) parties. There are plenty of reasons for us voters across the political spectrum to feel this way. Unbelievably only 18% of the money spent in US Congressional House races comes from within the Congressional district now, meaning over 80% comes from outside the district. Twenty-five years ago, the vast majority of these funds came from within the district.[89] This lends credence to the idea that your congressperson has more stake in representing the interests of their large donors than in representing your interests. And direct political giving is just part of the story. So-called super PACs can spend unlimited amounts to support or oppose candidates as long as they "don't coordinate with the campaign." In 2024 megadonors giving over $5 million each provided more than 75% of the funding to super PACs supporting major presidential candidates. And it's not just federal campaigns. "Outside" money can be even more influential in local and state elections. What to the rich are relatively small amounts of money can completely dominate local elections.

Does it work? The better-financed candidate in US House races wins over 90% of the time, and 70% to 88% of the time in Senate races, based on data from recent election cycles.[90] None of this is surprising. As normal citizens, most of us can't keep close track of what our representatives do. But

....

89 https://thehill.com/opinion/campaign/5457720-election-costs-rise-billions.

90 https://www.opensecrets.org/elections-overview/winning-vs-spending#:~:text=Money%20doesn't%20always%20equal,but%20applies%20in%20both%20chambers.

big-money donors, both individual and corporate, are well briefed on how legislators support their interests, and have legions of lobbyists to influence the drafting of legislation. Candidates who support their interests are well financed and supported through "independent" super PAC spending that often tars their opponents. Ads by these groups don't say "support candidate X (their compliant candidate) because he voted to make corporate jets tax-deductible"; they say "don't support candidate Y (a non-compliant candidate) because he'll vote for transgender bathrooms"—even if candidate Y has never said anything of the kind.[91] It's not just ads, of course. Well-paid operators influence elections through social media, and well-paid talking heads find it profitable to amplify the current distractions. This has been going on for a long time. Here's a quote from a biography of Reagan about his primary campaign against Gerald Ford:

> Like other conservative activists such as Richard Viguerie (dubbed the "King Midas of the New Right"), Howard Phillips, and Paul Weyrich, Helms and Ellis pioneered the use of direct-mail fundraising that kept donations coming in by frightening the faithful about purported Democratic plots to destroy America. "The shriller you are," one fundraiser noted, "the easier it is to raise money."[92]

Of course, these kinds of techniques have always been used in politics across the spectrum, but what is new now is the dominance of ultrarich ultraright big-money donors and their success. To repeat Warren Buffett's quote: "There's class warfare, all right. But it's my class, the rich class, that's making war, and we're winning."

The current Trump administration offers a master class in how the rich right uses social issues to advance its economic agenda. In 2024, polling indicated that immigration, trans rights, and inflation were hot-button issues, and these issues were liberally used in negative ads by dark money groups supporting Republican and MAGA candidates. They also threw in dark intimations about crime and creeping socialism. Project 2025, the Heritage Foundation blueprint for the next "conservative" presidency, also

91 Making corporate jets a tax write-off was a feature of the "Big Beautiful Bill".
92 Max Boot, *Reagan: His Life and Legend* (op. cit.) p. 531.

included widely unpopular ideas, so Trump, who is an excellent politician, distanced himself from that. As with Reagan, the Heritage Foundation had a major influence in Trump's first administration but was somewhat kept in check by more moderate voices, except for the 2017 tax cuts for corporations and the rich. The Heritage Foundation learned from that experience, and Project 2025 called for immediately putting loyalists in all the top positions and a great many second-rung ones. As soon as he assumed office the second time, Trump basically turned over the federal government to the Heritage Foundation. He appointed Russell Vought, one of Project 2025's chief architects and authors, to head the Office of Management and Budget, which basically runs everything now since the Supreme Court has freed the executive to override Congress on spending. Top personnel are chosen from lists of Heritage-vetted conservatives. To push through as much of their agenda as possible, Project 2025 called for almost dictatorial presidential power, which is daily being tested in the courts and generally upheld by a compliant Supreme Court. The beneficiaries of all this are certainly not working people, and certainly not the young. But the rich mega donors behind the Heritage Foundation have gained mightily.

The 2025 "Big Beautiful Bill" made the 2017 Trump/Heritage tax cuts permanent. Those tax cuts gave the largest dollar and *percentage* cuts to those in the top 5% and did so by increasing the deficit.[93] The bill was full of special interest pork, especially for the fossil fuel industry, one of the biggest contributors to the Heritage Foundation. There was also pork for the alcohol industry, private equity fund managers, and wealthy heirs.

In the second Trump administration those tax cuts have been made permanent, adding an estimated $4.2 trillion to the national debt over four years. But Project 2025's "Big Beautiful Bill" recoups about a billion of that by cutting Medicaid, SNAP, and student loans among other things, so it will "only" add about $3.2 trillion to the deficit over ten years. The young, including the yet-to-be-born, and those in the bottom 50% of income, will be the biggest losers and old rich people the biggest winners, according to

....

93 https://www.americanprogress.org/article/the tax cuts-and-jobs-act-failed-to-deliver-promised-benefits.

the Penn Wharton Budget Model.[94]

Meanwhile a program of distraction has been put in place. Trump is a master of distraction. Tariffs! Deportations! DEI! DOGE! National Guard to blue cities to fight nonexistent crime waves! Department of War! Gulf of America! Daily Executive Orders! Christians Being Persecuted! Antifa! "Enemies within"! Tylenol causes autism! You name it.

How is Trump/Heritage doing on the other hot-button social issues we've noted? On immigration there is a lot of noise, but no immigration reform bill has been proposed or enacted. That means that about 66,000 legal immigrants enter the country every month, or about 800,000 per year. Border control does need to be maintained, but we've shown that immigration is not a serious economic problem, and anyone who subscribes to the idea that we should reduce legal immigration should note that this runs counter to business interests and won't happen.[95]

How about prices? They keep going up, and now import prices are going up because of tariffs. Those tariffs are a tax, paid by US consumers, that the federal government collects, to the tune of $31 billion a month currently. That somewhat offsets the income and corporate tax cuts for the rich, but a tariff, like a sales tax, falls mostly on the middle class and poor.[96]

Questions of identity and values are not of much economic importance and so keeping the base(s) happy costs the rich nothing. Those issues fall more in the realm of core beliefs, so the Cato Institute—which is libertarian and for individual freedom—feels differently about transgender rights and abortion (issues of individual freedom) than the evangelicals and Christian nationalists.

In short, Trump and the Republican Congress got elected on social issues as well as economic ones. On the social issues they cater to the base(s) when it costs the rich nothing, while on the economic issues they have delivered

....

94 https://budgetmodel.wharton.upenn.edu/issues/2025/7/8/president-trump-signed-reconciliation-bill-budget-economic-and-distributional-effects (amusingly, Penn Wharton is Trump's alma mater).

95 There is a misperception that legal immigration rules have changed under Trump 2. They haven't.

96 The rich tend to invest a larger share of their income, increasing their wealth further. The poor and middle class spend more of their income. Thus sales taxes and tariffs which, unlike income taxes, are not scaled to income fall heaviest on lower incomes.

additional huge tax cuts for the rich and higher prices for everyone. They are also cutting Medicaid, SNAP, student loans, and other programs that serve lower-income people. As Doctor Phil used to ask, "How's that working out for you?"

One of the most broken things in the US is this economic and political takeover by the ultrarich ultraright. Follow the money. It is high time we, the people, take back the country. It won't be easy with all the distraction, but there's nothing like a $10,000 increase in your health insurance to focus attention. To start with, no representative who voted for the Big Beautiful Bill should be returned to Congress. Vote for someone, of any political party or an independent, who shares your values but hasn't sold out to big money.

TAX THE RICH

Thanks to the Supreme Court, there is very little we can do currently to keep big money out of politics. That is a longer-term problem that may require a Constitutional amendment. In the meantime, we must be savvy about who we vote for and understand the forces at play. But there is plenty we can do to reduce lopsided income and wealth inequality. This book of course advocates for Shares in America, which would increase income taxes on the wealthy and transfer that income to those with lower incomes. I'd like to point out that plenty of well-off and rich people support increasing taxes on the wealthy. In an op-ed he titled "Stop Coddling the Super-Rich," Warren Buffett pointed out that in 2010 he paid around $7 million in income taxes.[97] While that sounds like a lot of money, it was only 17% of his taxable income, whereas everyone else in his office paid a much higher percentage. Why do the rich pay much less in taxes as a percentage of income than the middle class? Because of tax laws that highly favor the wealthy. As we've pointed out, the rich pay little to no payroll tax, one of the largest taxes. The tax on "unearned" income such as capital gains is about 15%, which is lower than the tax on earned income in many cases. Mr. Buffet, who knows about this

97 https://www.nytimes.com/2011/00/15/opinion/stop-coddling-the-super-rich.html.

stuff, provides some examples of how the tax code has been twisted to favor the rich in his op ed. An organization called Patriotic Millionaires often calls for taxing the rich more, noting that unearned income is taxed at lower rates than wages. Bill Gates has joined Buffet in calling for higher capital gains tax rates and higher estate taxes. Higher estate taxes are essential to deal with the truly mind-boggling inequality of wealth in the US. It really is true that three men owned more wealth than the bottom 50% of Americans in 2018.[98] Why should the children of the wealthy inherit huge fortunes they didn't create? I have nothing against Bezos enjoying the great wealth he built, but why should that pass on to his children? Realistically, if you can pass on a few million dollars to each of your kids, great. But beyond that, no. As Bill Gates has said, "It's not a favor to kids to have them have huge sums of wealth. It distorts anything they might do, creating their own path."[99] And it certainly isn't fair to the homeless kid. High marginal income tax rates and inheritance taxes could be designed to ensure that vast wealth is not passed on from generation to generation.[100]

Taxing all income the same, whether it's earned through a paycheck or as a dividend on a stock, or from selling shares, or from an inheritance, seems fair. Combined with high marginal tax rates, such a universal income tax could greatly reduce income inequality immediately and wealth inequality over time. Such a reform would increase taxes only at the top of the income pyramid and would pay for Shares in America with plenty left over to reduce the deficit. The US federal tax code is 7,000 pages long. Presidents have repeatedly run on simplifying it and removing loopholes, and yet more loopholes keep being added. We can't look at detailed tax reform here, but it's time to get it done.

---

98 https://www.forbes.com/sites/noahkirsch/2017/11/09/the-3-richest-americans-hold-more-wealth-than-bottom-50-of-country-study-finds.

99 https://wror.com/2023/09/30/mick-jagger-bill-gates-may-not-leave-massive-inheritance.

100 The Economist recently published an editorial titled "The return of inheritocracy" https://www.economist.com/leaders/2025/02/27/inheriting-is-becoming-nearly-as-important-as-working.

REDUCE INCOME AND WEALTH INEQUALITY

I've already argued for Shares in America as the best way to reduce income inequality. But there are other ways to reduce income inequality, and even Shares in America might not be enough unless it is sufficiently large. A $1,000-per-month-per-adult share would leave a single adult, who is unable to work for whatever reason, below the poverty line. That means we'd continue to have other transfers, such as housing and food subsidies, in place, as well as disability insurance, which is unfortunately subject to abuse by both individuals and states seeking to pass welfare costs on to the federal government. In the sample Shares in America™ program I outlined above (see Figure 21), I left all the current means-tested programs in place and at current levels. If Shares offsets benefits, the people who need it most won't get the full income boost. To ensure that everyone receives a full benefit, Shares should not be included as income in tax or benefit calculations. It would be best if we could eliminate means-tested programs almost entirely which argues for raising the Share in America basic income so that people no longer need the support of means-tested programs to get by. The higher the basic income, the more such programs can be reduced and the tax money spent on them used instead to fund Shares. Some of the "tech bros" think a minimum $2,000 per month UBI is required. But we could start with a lower amount and work up over time.

The alternative, adopted broadly in Europe, is a more generous safety net, some of it means-tested, some of it not. As long as the rich are taxed more, and the benefits flow broadly to the public and especially to lower-income people, then such a safety net also reduces income inequality. Some examples: unemployment insurance varies by state in the US and depends on your past earnings. Maximum benefits range from $235 in Mississippi to $1,015 in Massachusetts, with an average of about $400 a week for 26 weeks in 2022. In Germany jobless benefit pays 60% of previous salary for a year. France provides up to 75% of the previous average daily wage for up to two years. In Europe, health coverage is universal. Britain's National Health Service, which is funded by taxes and offers free care to everyone, costs the government 7% of GDP per year. In contrast, healthcare costs 17.6% of GDP in the US, over $13,000 per person in 2023, and is only partially subsidized. Under the Big Beautiful Bill healthcare subsidies are being cut. Healthcare is a special issue: it is not subject to supply and demand the way other goods and services are. Amazingly, in the US, you can be denied life-saving cancer treatment if you can't pay for it. In no other advanced country is that the case. Universal coverage lowers costs, and it does not require a single-payer approach. A report by the Kaiser Family Foundation notes that:

> The US health system is fragmented, with many private and public payers, and with regulation of these payers split between states and the federal government. However, these features are not entirely unique to the US, either. Indeed, some other countries with much lower health spending have multiple private payers or differences in public programs across states or provinces. The US is also not alone in having a mainly fee-for-service payment system.[101]

In the US, medical care costs for the same services have risen much more slowly under Medicare and Medicaid than for private insurance, strongly suggesting that the best way to keep costs under control is through universal coverage. This is one safety net program that has to be maintained if for no other reason than costs and cost increases are unsustainable. As the population ages and demand increases the problem only gets worse. We should follow the lead of other countries that provide universal coverage while keeping costs down. We in the US spend nearly twice as much as the average of comparable countries: $13,432 vs $7,393 per person. And the data is clear that universal coverage improves health outcomes as well as costs.[102] The US performs worse than the average developed nation on 77% of health status indicators like life expectancy, obesity, and opioid mortality rate, according to an Organization for Economic Cooperation and Development report.[103]

While Shares in America complements programs like Social Security, it could eventually replace most other welfare. At the outset, Shares would not be counted as income for determining eligibility for means-tested benefits,

101 https://www.kff.org/health-costs/health-policy-101-health-care-costs-and-affordability/?entry=table-of-contents-what-factors-contribute-to-u-s-health-care-spending.

102 https://www.healthsystemtracker.org.

103 https://www.oecd.org/en/topics/health.html.

ensuring no one loses support during the transition. The Earned Income Tax Credit and Child Tax Credit could be fully replaced, as they are essentially similar forms of cash transfers (the "means-tested" income limit for the Child Tax Credit is $400,000 under the Big Beautiful Bill). As Shares rise to levels sufficient to lift people well above poverty, other programs such as fuel assistance and SNAP could be reduced or phased out, simplifying the system. Health insurance, however, should be universal and provided as a right to every American.

TONE DOWN THE CULTURE WAR

When I was a teenager my sister, who loved horses, worked at a stable not far from our house. Some of the horses were let out by the hour and riders were taken on tours of a local forest preserve. I went on a number of such rides and noticed that some horses would insist on a "pecking order": if another horse tried to pass one of these it would neigh and snap at the offender. For me, it was a kind of parable. Here we humans were riding the horses, and they were fighting among themselves.

So, it is with us: we fight among ourselves while being fleeced by the rich. Keeping us riled up at each other distracts us from our common interests. As I mentioned at the start of this chapter, income and wealth inequality, money in politics, and partisanship are highly interrelated in the US today. The connection is not hard to follow: Increased income and wealth inequality has driven money in politics, which uses divisive techniques to elect compliant politicians, who pass legislation that enriches the rich further. A nice feedback loop which has worked amazingly well.

It is unrealistic to expect us all to get along on everything. Social strife is as old as the hills and certainly a recurrent theme in US history. The Revolution was no picnic: it pitted loyalists against patriots, and they killed each other with abandon. The early republic pitted Federalists against Tories and there were physical brawls in Congress. The Civil War was driven by absolutist religious fervor: each side claimed God was on their side, although, as usual, following the money tells much of the story. The Progressive Era and Prohibition were rife with passion. Passion and varied beliefs are normal; in a healthy democracy we debate issues and come to arrangements consistent with our core principles as laid out in the Constitution and its amendments. Partisan gridlock occurs when one side or both refuse to engage in normal political give-and-take. That can happen when one political group labels another as "the enemy within," which calls to mind war, civil or otherwise, rather than democratic engagement. Such a fever pitch of undemocratic fervor is just about always the result of intentional stoking of passions, with the goal being power or economic gain, or both. President Trump recently addressed a convocation of top generals at the Pentagon and darkly referred to using the military to practice on "the enemy within." A retired general remarked "The enemy within isn't the military. And it isn't the American people. So, who is it?"

We've seen that money in politics has done much of the partisan stoking in recent decades. Here's a quote from the introduction to Heritage's Project 2025:

> "The long march of cultural Marxism through our institutions has come to pass. The federal government is a behemoth, weaponized against American citizens and conservative values, with freedom and liberty under siege as never before."

As we've seen, by far the federal government's largest expenditures are Social Security and Medicare followed by Medicaid, the military, and the national debt. "Cultural Marxism" is a made-up term which tries to tie cultural difference to economics. Marxism is an economic system and has nothing to do with cultural issues. Does anyone really think we're a Marxist country economically? In any case the language used is hardly what one would expect from a tax-deductible 501(c)(3) "charitable organization" supposedly engaged in serious thought. There are many such examples in Project 2025.

The rise of partisan media has also been polarizing and tends to create "tribalism": if you're a member of the "tribe" you subscribe to a whole menu of positions that contrasts with another "tribe." One of the contributing factors was the rise of 24-hour cable news: Cable news channels like Fox

News and MSNBC played a major role in normalizing partisan journalism. They blur the line between news and opinion, relying on commentators and pundits to attract and retain ideologically aligned viewers for ratings and profit. Research has shown that Fox News's slanted coverage, in particular, has led viewers to learn a biased set of facts.[104]

In other words, dividing and polarizing pays well. We see that even in religion these days. It's literally like an addictive drug: It lights up the same part of your brain as heroin.

Despite all of the above, I am thoroughly optimistic about us as a people, especially the great middle of Americans. I firmly believe that, like me, most Americans are committed to maintaining democracy in this country—and to the respectful negotiation of differences through the political process. We have seen that "red" voters will vote for a Democrat who shares their cultural values and represents their economic interests, and vice-versa. There are "red" states with "blue" governors and "blue" states with "red" governors. These governors tend to be moderates, not hardline ideologues; we must all allow for a "big tent." The American public is far less partisan than one would think from the media: Elections tend to go back and forth between parties, and the popular vote in the presidential elections has been close and swinging as well. I'm thoroughly optimistic about our country staying "of the people and by the people" and continuing as the longest-running constitutional democracy in history.

MAKING IT SO

Political Action

Staying abreast of which politician stands for what policy and how they actually vote is difficult for us regular citizens. Special interests, such as

---

104 There are multiple sources for this. David E. Broockman and Joshua Kalla, 2023, "The manifold effects of partisan media on viewers' beliefs and attitudes: A field experiment with Fox News viewers"; Homa Hosseinmardi, Samuel Wolken, David M. Rothschild, and Duncan J. Watts, 2025, "Unpacking Media Bias in the Growing Divide between Cable and Network News." *Scientific Reports* 15 (1): 17607.; and others

corporations and the rich, know all about legislation affecting them; in fact they often take a hand in drafting it. They also know exactly how politicians vote on issues of financial concern to them. There are over 12,000 lobbyists in Washington, DC, and a similar number at the state level. Regular voters have economic interests too! If you would like to see Shares in America become a reality and are fed up with money-soaked politics, please sign up as a supporter and register for our newsletter. We will let you know which politicians and candidates support Shares in America and how they vote on economic and money-in-politics issues. If you are a politician who supports Shares in America, let us know that too. You can sign up by going to our website at https://SharesInAmerica.com.

Social issues are not our concern; they can be debated elsewhere. We welcome politicians and voters regardless of party who share our views on economic issues.

The battle ahead won't be easy. Money is so firmly entrenched in politics and so effective in its ability to sway elections that reversing the tide will require a long-term extended effort. In that effort we all need to do our part or lose our country as a democracy.

Religion's Role

One last appeal is to the religious. I'm not qualified to make theological arguments, but religion has played, and continues to play, a large role in shaping politics. The Civil War and Progressive movement both had religious moral imperatives for many. Personally, I'm not religious in a fundamentalist sense, but I believe that religion provides a valuable framework for moral discussion. So, I'm just going to mention some biblical quotes.

"No one can serve two masters; for a slave will either hate the one and love the other, or be devoted to the one and despise the other. You cannot serve God and wealth." Matthew 6:24

"How hard it will be for those who have wealth to enter the kingdom of God! … It is easier for a camel to go through the eye of a needle than for someone who is rich to enter the kingdom of God." Mark 10:23–25

"He has told you, O mortal, what is good; and what does the Lord require of you but to do justice, and to love kindness, and to walk humbly with your God?" Micah 6:8

"Then there is the Jubilee's universally ignored call for redistribution of wealth, land at the time, every 50 years, noting that God owns the land ultimately." Leviticus 25

And in Corinthians 13 we have this beautiful passage:

> If I speak in the tongues of men or of angels, but do not have love, I am only a resounding gong or a clanging cymbal. If I have the gift of prophecy and can fathom all mysteries and all knowledge, and if I have a faith that can move mountains, but do not have love, I am nothing. If I give all I possess to the poor and give over my body to hardship that I may boast, but do not have love, I gain nothing.
>
> Love is patient, love is kind. It does not envy, it does not boast, it is not proud. It does not dishonor others, it is not self-seeking it is not easily angered, it keeps no record of wrongs. Love does not delight in evil but rejoices with the truth. It always protects, always trusts, always hopes, always perseveres.
>
> Love never fails. But where there are prophecies, they will cease; where there are tongues, they will be stilled; where there is knowledge, it will pass away. For we know in part and we prophesy in part, but when completeness comes, what is in part disappears. When I was a child, I talked like a child, I thought like a child, I reasoned like a child. When I became a man, I put the ways of childhood behind me. For now we see only a reflection as in a mirror; then we shall see face to face. Now I know in part; then I shall know fully, even as I am fully known.
>
> And now these three remain: faith, hope, and love. But the greatest of these is love.

Religious communities too, need to do their part. Preaching hate is unacceptable. Advocating for the poor and greater economic equality would seem to be in line with core teachings.

Some Inspiring Quotes

"The greatest source of instability in constitutions is the disproportion between rich and poor." Aristotle, Greek Philosopher (c. 400 BCE)

"We may have democracy, or we may have wealth concentrated in the hands of a few, but we cannot have both." Louis Brandeis, US Supreme Court justice (1856–1941)

A State divided into a small number of rich and a large number of poor will always develop a government manipulated by the rich to protect the amenities represented by their property." Harold Laski, British political theorist (1893–1950)

"The poor have sometimes objected to being governed badly. The rich have always objected to being governed at all." G. K. Chesterton, English essayist (1874–1936)

"How does one put together a democracy based on the concept of equality while running an economy with ever greater degrees of economic inequality?" Lester Thurow, American economist (1938–2016)

CODA AND SUMMARY

The United States is an amazingly successful country.

At the dawn of the twentieth century, most Americans lived lives that were physically demanding, materially modest, and often precarious. In 1900, the average person could expect to live less than fifty years. Infectious disease was a leading cause of death; few homes had electricity or running water; and child labor, racial segregation, and poverty were widespread. Over the past century and a quarter, the United States has undergone a transformation so deep that daily life would be almost unrecognizable to someone from that earlier era.

The most profound change has been in health. Public sanitation, clean water, vaccination, antibiotics, and modern medicine raised life expectancy by more than thirty years and nearly eliminated many once-common diseases. Childbirth has become vastly safer, and infant mortality has dropped by more than 90%.

Material well-being has expanded in equal measure. Real income per person is roughly six times higher than in 1900, and basic comforts once reserved for the wealthy—electric lights, indoor plumbing, refrigerators, heating, and air conditioning—has become standard. The spread of automobiles, airplanes, computers, and the internet has revolutionized work, communication, and leisure. Americans now enjoy far greater access to food, shelter, information, and entertainment than any previous generation.

Education has opened doors that were previously closed to most. At the start of the century, fewer than 1 in 10 young Americans finished high school; today, 9 in 10 do, and millions attend college. Universal literacy, public libraries, and digital technology put an unprecedented range of knowledge within reach of everyone.

The expansion of rights has been just as striking. Women gained the vote in 1920; civil rights legislation in the 1960s ended legal segregation; and later movements extended recognition to people with disabilities and to the LGBTQ+ community. Laws protecting workers, banning child labor, and setting minimum wages reshaped the conditions of employment. Americans today benefit from social safety nets—Social Security, unemployment insurance, Medicare, and Medicaid—that did not exist in 1900 and that protect millions from destitution.

Science and technology have powered this transformation. Electrification, mechanized farming, and modern industry have made food and manufactured goods abundant. Environmental awareness has also grown: conservation efforts created national parks, and later laws such as the Clean Air and Clean Water Acts made urban life healthier and more sustainable.

We've come a long way since the late 1800s, when the wealthy robber barons of industry and finance dominated the economy and largely controlled the government. Much of that progress came through reforms the rich right derided as "socialist." If it had been up to the robber barons, we would still be working twelve hours a day, six days a week, for miserable wages. We wouldn't have the right to unionize, there would be no Social Security or Medicare, cigarettes and asbestos would still be advertised as healthy, and factories would continue to pour toxic smoke into the air and dump waste into our rivers.

The dire predictions made by corporate leaders about these reforms never came true. Instead, the nation built a robust middle class that fueled a virtuous cycle of consumption and growth. But by the early 1970s, our success in producing more with less labor began to reverse the postwar trend toward greater equality. Technology-driven productivity gains in agriculture and manufacturing steadily reduced the demand for general labor, leading to job losses, regional decline, and falling wages for many.

At the same time—beginning around the Reagan era—the rich right and corporate interests launched a sustained campaign to demonize government, discredit reformers, cut taxes for the wealthy, weaken unions, and turn Americans against one another for political gain. That campaign succeeded. Today, the new "robber barons" of finance, industry, and high tech once again dominate both the economy and government—and they are unimaginably richer now.

So how do we, the people, fight back? By voting. We are still a democracy, and we could, within a few election cycles, replace nearly all our elected officials with those who actually represent our interests. But that requires two things: candidates who reject the influence of big money and a clear program they can unite behind. It won't be easy though; money is very effective in politics. Even the handful of congresspeople who have pledged not to take PAC money, 11 Democrats and 2 Republicans by one count, can find themselves up against unlimited negative spending by dark-money super PACs. Money in politics must be one of our main targets. Supreme Court decisions have made this a long-term struggle—one that may ultimately require a constitutional amendment or a change in the court's composition—but we can start now. Candidates should pledge not to take Super PAC money and to work toward restoring limits on political spending.

More immediately Congress can increase taxes on the well-off, as many wealthy Americans have themselves suggested. We must reduce the deficit instead of expanding it; otherwise, we're passing an unsustainable burden to future generations. Medical care costs must be brought under control and insurance made universal. We must simplify the 7,000-page tax code and eliminate loopholes. And we must reduce rising income and wealth inequality.

Shares in America provides a way forward. It would allow every American to share in the nation's growth and prosperity while giving us the flexibility to adjust payments as technology continues to reshape the economy. The United States is an extraordinarily rich nation, generating over $190,000 in net income per household each year. It truly has the potential to be a great country for all. We just need to make it so.

APPENDIX A
GRAPH AND DATA SOURCES

Almost all the graphs in this book were generated by the author from the best available data sources, including the Bureau of Labor Statistics (BLS), Bureau of Economic Analysis (BEA) which publishes the US National Accounts (NIPA) tables, the Census Bureau—including the American Community Survey (ACS), the Congressional Budget Office (CBO), the World Inequality Database (WID), and the Federal Reserve (FED). Many of these organizations provide interfaces for retrieving and downloading data. The Federal Reserve aggregates a lot of data from many sources and provides an excellent easy-to-use application for graphing this data and downloading it called FRED. I often developed the graphs first using FRED, which is available at https://fred.stlouisfed.org/.

For transparency, I I have provided a list of all the graphs and other images along with their data sources and in some cases links to the actual spreadsheets used to create the basic graphics. You can find these at https://SharesInAmerica.com/book.

I have also provided an extensive bibliography at that site.

APPENDIX B
THE USE OF AI IN THE BOOK

Every word in this book was written by the author unless noted otherwise. That said, AI was helpful in doing research in the same way that internet search engines still are. I used ChatGPT and, since Google provides AI search summaries by default, I looked at those as well. But it became very clear to me that AI is no substitute for deep research. I found myself reading lengthy books to feel confident writing a few pages of text, unless of course I was already thoroughly versed in the subject. But ChatGPT was very helpful in condensing a subject to provide a framework for research and answered detailed technical questions about statistics that might otherwise take hours to ferret out of technical documentation. I always check any information provided by AI, as should we all. Google's search summary told me that Reagan was first inaugurated in 1980, although that now seems to have been fixed. For overviews of many issues I found Wikipedia very helpful, again as a summary source for further research, and was pleasantly surprised by the depth of discussion and information available in Reddit in such subreddits as AskHistorians. In addition to the aforementioned lengthy books, I also read countless academic papers. There is nothing like a varied diet to develop a discriminating palate, but in the end, you must process everything like a detective solving a complicated case to arrive at a picture of reality.

By the way, the em dashes were added by my copy editor. I never knew they existed.

ABOUT THE AUTHOR

Richard Frenkel gained his understanding of economics in both academic settings (at Boston University and MIT) and in real-world jobs (including working in a shoe factory, managing in the corporate world, and running a profitable IT firm). He's written reports for MIT's Center for Policy Alternatives and several books about world and US economics.

A longtime resident of Swampscott, Massachusetts, Richard regularly participates in town meetings and committees, where nonpartisan civic engagement is alive and well. He strongly believes that Americans can make our future better. He'd love to hear from you at **SharesInAmerica.com**.

INDEX

L

labor. *See also* unions
    during COVID, 42
    demand and supply factors. *see also*
      productivity growth22, 45
    falling demand for, 22, 45
    technology and, 66, 87, 118
labor costs, minimization of, 88–89
labor force participation rate, 43, *43*
labor laws, 52, 56
Labor Relations Act, 56
Laski, Harold, 142
"lean manufacturing," 40
Lewis, Sinclair, 31
Lindert, Peter, 10
livable basic income (LBI), 68
lobbying, 73–74, *74*, 140
low-income households, 16–17

M

MAGA, 130–131
making it so, 140–142
managed capitalism, 88–89, 94
Manhattan Institute, 81
manufacturing, 44, 50
    apparel manufacturing, 24–26, 27
    "bringing back," 88–91
    declining employment in, 22–23, *23*,
      24–29, 30, 45, 61, 66, 86, 89–91
    "lean manufacturing," 40
    modernization of, 145
    productivity growth and, 10–14
    "reshored" jobs, 89
    tariffs to "bring back," 87, 88–91
    trade deficit and, 29–30
market economies, 88–89
Marxism, 138
Massachusetts, 135
material well-being, 144
Mayors for a Guaranteed Income, 123–124
McCarthy, Joseph, 59
McCarthyism, 77
McCormick reaper, 6
McKinley, William, 53, 75
McKinsey & Company, 122

means-tested programs, 15, 98, 99, 103,
    116, 117, 135
meatpacking industry, 30, 31, 32
media conglomeration, 20, 109. *See also*
    cable news channels
Medicaid, 14–15, 17, 63, 65, 78, 84, 87, 109,
    111, 117–118, 131, 133, 136, 138, 145
Medicare, 14–15, 63, 65, 67, 78, 82, 87, 109,
    111, 136, 138, 145
Medicare Prescription Drug Act, 82
men, in the labor force, 43, 44
Mercatus Center, George Mason
    University, 76
Michelin, 27
middle class, 58, 86
    black, 65
    building of, 145
    expanding, 58
    GI Bill and, 95
    shrinking, 44, 98
the Midwest, 27
migrants, undocumented, 92–93
minimum wage, 24, 52, 56, 67, 80
misinformation, 127
Mississippi, 135
money in politics, 126–132, 140, 146
monopoly pricing, 49–50
Motor Vehicle Air Pollution Control Act of
    1965, 63
MSNBC, 138
Murray, Charles, 81–82
Musk, Elon, 83, 124
Muskie, Edmund, 67

N

Nader, Ralph, 70
NAFTA (North American Free Trade
    Agreement), 23, 73
NASA (National Aeronautics and Space
    Administration), 12
National Endowment for the Arts (NEA),
    63
national health insurance, 58, 65, 67, 82,
    135–136
National Health Service, 135–136